ALL THE WILD HORSES

I WAS IN NORTHERN NEVADA back in 1987 buying feeder cattle to stock my ranch in Oregon, when I passed a government wild-horse holding facility in Lovelock. The corrals were packed with unhappy mustangs standing in boredom—gaunt ribbed, heads hanging in sleepy stupor, lips drooping, eyes half closed against swarms of flies. As a young cowboy in the 1930s, I grew up with wild horses in Oregon. I have loved them since my boyhood as they've given me great joy—from the first young mustang I trained and rode out on the range, to the bands running free about me, adding their beauty to an already fabulous landscape. Now, seeing these captive wild horses, my old cowboy heart ached. For a moment I thought I owed it to them to sneak up in the dead of night, open the gates, and let the horses run to freedom. But the horses had been gathered because of chronic drought and a lack of food on their ranges. I knew setting these wild horses free again would accomplish nothing.

As I stood watching the captured animals, my thoughts went back to World War II. In 1944, I was on a troop train traveling east across the Nevada desert, headed toward the East Coast, where I would embark for the European theater of war. East of Winnemucca, the engineer sounded a steam whistle that startled a bunch of wild horses, and for perhaps twenty miles they galloped beside the train. I could not help but think they were saying goodbye to me personally, and when they finally veered off north toward the mountains, I took off my hat to them and was lonelier than ever.

Most of a lifetime later, as I looked over the fence at those poor, captive mustangs, I wondered if any of them were descendants of the horses who raced my troop train more than half a century before.

In minutes, I was on the telephone to my children in Oregon asking them to take over the ranch. I was leaving on an adventure that was to consume my life: I was bound and determined to set up a sanctuary for wild horses that would allow them to run wild and free. ⚘

Dayton O. Hyde

ALL THE WILD HORSES

Preserving the Spirit and Beauty of the World's Wild Horses

DAYTON O. HYDE

Founder of the
Black Hills Wild Horse Sanctuary

Photography by Rita Summers
& Charles G. Summers, Jr.

Voyageur
Press

WE WOULD LIKE TO THANK the many people who share our interest in wild horses and have been helpful in sharing their knowledge. First, George Evans of Baggs, Wyoming, who showed us our first wild horses on the plains of southern Wyoming on an exciting ride in remote country where the horses feel safe. Thanks also to the Rock Springs BLM wranglers who care for wild horses, especially Jim Williams, Vic McDermott, and Bobby Anderson.

Our introduction to the wild horses in Namibia was with a remarkable man, Tommy Hall, who was working as a conservation officer in area at that time. Tommy has become a good friend, and we have returned to watch the wild horses with him several times.

Thanks also to the wonderful ranchers in the Camargue region of France who were so kind in helping us get photographs of the beautiful horses of that region: Jean-Luc Malacarne with La Maison du Cheval de Camargue and Jean-Pierre Persch.

A special thanks to Dayton Hyde, who has dedicated his life to saving wild horses on his beautiful sanctuary in South Dakota. His knowledge of horses and love of the wild horse is an inspiration to us. Equally dedicated is Susan Watt, manager of the Black Hills Wild Horse Sanctuary, who also supplied immeasurable help and hospitality.

*As long as wild horses are galloping free
I'll dream of the West as I want it to be.* 🐎

—Rita and Charlie Summers

First published in 2006 by Voyageur Press, an imprint of MBI Publishing Company, Galtier Plaza, Suite 200, 380 Jackson Street, St. Paul, MN 55101-3885 USA

Text copyright © 2006 by Dayton O. Hyde

Photography copyright © 2006 by Rita Summers and Charles G. Summers, Jr.

Photography pages 71-77 and 92-93 copyright © 2006 by Animal Photography

All rights reserved. With the exception of quoting brief passages for the purposes of review, no part of this publication may be reproduced without prior written permission from the Publisher. The information in this book is true and complete to the best of our knowledge. All recommendations are made without any guarantee on the part of the author or Publisher, who also disclaim any liability incurred in connection with the use of this data or specific details. We recognize, further, that some words, model names, and designations mentioned herein are the property of the trademark holder. We use them for identification purposes only. This is not an official publication.

MBI Publishing Company titles are also available at discounts in bulk quantity for industrial or sales-promotional use. For details write to Special Sales Manager at MBI Publishing Company, Galtier Plaza, Suite 200, 380 Jackson Street, St. Paul, MN 55101-3885 USA

ISBN-13: 978-0-7603-2590-2
ISBN-10: 0-7603-2590-1

Library of Congress Cataloging-in-Publication Data

Hyde, Dayton O., 1925-
   All the wild horses : preserving the spirit and beauty of the world's wild horses / by Dayton O. Hyde ; photography by Rita Summers and Charles G. Summers, Jr.
      p. cm.
   ISBN-13: 978-0-7603-2590-2 (plc w/ jacket)
   ISBN-10: 0-7603-2590-1 (plc w/ jacket)
   1. Wild horses. 2. Wild horses—Pictorial works. I. Summers, Rita. II. Summers, Charles G., 1936- III. Title.
   SF360.H93 2006
   599.665'50222--dc22
                                    2006015586

Editor: Michael Dregni
Designer: Rochelle Schultz Brancato

Printed in Hong Kong

On page 1: Wild stallion, Carmody Lake, Wyoming.

On pages 4-5: A wild herd charges through sage and snow at Elk Horn Spring, Wyoming.

On page 6: Clockwise from top left, Medicine Hat paint, Black Hills Wild Horse Sanctuary; Pryor Mountain foal, Montana; Palomino cremelo stallion, Arrowhead Mountain, Montana; Pyzewalski horse.

On page 7: The Camargue wild horse in France.

On page 8: A bay runs through the sagebrush on Green Mountain, Wyoming.

On page 9: Young stallions spar on Arrowhead Mountain, Wyoming.

On page 10: Outer Banks wild horses at Corolla, North Carolina.

On page 11: A wild horse in the Namib Desert, Aus, Namibia.

On the title pages: Sulphur stallion, Utah.

Inset on the title page: A wild horse saunters across the plains at Carmody Lake, Wyoming.

On the contents page: 1. Fighting Namibian stallions in Africa. 2. Wild horses before the Outer Banks surf at Corolla, North Carolina. 3. Camargue stallion with mares in France. 4. A plains Zebra herd drinking at Etosha National Park, Namibia.

A COLORFUL HERD OF WILD HORSES RUSHES ACROSS A MEADOW
ON GREEN MOUNTAIN, WYOMING.

CONTENTS

1	WILD HORSES OF MY YOUNG COWBOY DAYS	19
2	A SHORT HISTORY OF THE LONG TRAIL OF THE HORSE	35
	Prehistory	35
	Indians and Wild Horses	37
3	WILD HORSES OF THE WORLD	43
	Zebras	43
	Wild Horses of the Namib Desert	62
	Wild Horses of the French Camargue	78
	Sorraia Mustangs	94
	Pryor Mountain Mustangs	94
	Kiger Mustangs	95
	Nokota Mustangs	95
	Wild Ponies of Chincoteague and Assateague	100

4	**PROTECTING OUR WILD HORSES**	115
	Home on the Range	115
	The Wild Horse and Burro Protection Act of 1971	117
	Where Wild Horses Run Free	118
5	**SEASONS ON THE WILD HORSE SANCTUARY**	133
	Winter	133
	Spring	144
	Summer	160
	Autumn	170
	Days of Wonder	186
6	**THE TRUE WORTH OF WILD HORSES**	195
	INDEX	206
	ABOUT THE AUTHORS	208

Chapter 1

WILD HORSES OF
MY YOUNG COWBOY DAYS

I FIRST CROSSED PATHS with wild horses on the Klamath Indian Reservation in southern Oregon where I was cowboying in the late 1930s. That same day, I also stumbled across a bootleg whiskey still hidden in a cluster of willows along the Williamson River—a stumble that could have been my last.

Just thirteen, I was riding for my uncle's cattle outfit, gathering any stray cattle that might have wandered into the hostile territory of neighboring ranges. The old man had warned me to keep eyes in the back of my head: There were neighbors who had done penitentiary time for rustling cattle—among other things—and might resent my poking around.

I was stealing a ride on a big bay horse named Sleepy, who, admittedly, was sometimes a little bit better at bucking than I was at riding. Sleepy had a way of coming awake at the least expected times, and now he suddenly shied at a shaft of sunlight reflected off a huge metal pot and a pile of whiskey bottles stashed in the brush. I pulled all the leather I could just to stay on when Sleepy made a massive leap eastward and left my cowboy hat hanging on a willow. I managed to retrieve my hat, and both the horse and I were relieved to cross the river and get out of there.

We had ridden about three miles through a forest of huge ponderosa pines when I heard some brush crackle and then the pounding of hooves—a herd of wild horses swept through the forest before us. An old bay mare led the way, followed by several mares heavy with foal. Then came a couple of sorrel yearlings trailing the herd, copper coats gleaming in the sun. They were as beautiful as any horses I had ever seen.

The old lead mare saw me, stopped dead in her tracks, then snorted in terror as she whirled and took her band up over the ridges. The dust had hardly settled when an Indian galloped up on a foam-flecked buckskin horse. His reata hung ready over his saddlehorn; already formed, the loop slapped against the buckskin's knees. The man's eyes showed his anger as he saw that the horses had spooked and headed up over the ridge.

"Damn," he cursed. "Almost had 'em to the river!"

I recognized him as the man my uncle had warned me about, but I was still mesmerized by seeing the wild band.

"Those two sorrels," I said. "You ever get them in, I want to buy them from you. And if you get them for me, I promise not to tell anyone about your still by the river."

Two weeks later I found the two sorrel mustangs haltered and tied to my uncle's corral fence. No one had seen the man come and go, but from the tracks it was clear he had taken one of my uncle's saddle horses with him as payment for the colts.

I christened those two sorrels Red and Willie, and they soon settled into life on a cattle ranch. It wasn't long before I was riding them out on the range on which they had been born. I often wondered what went on in the minds of those two horses as they bore me out across the forested ridges and green finger meadows where they had lived. Sometimes they paused unbidden at the edge of a meadow and stared into the distance as though looking for the band of mares that had birthed them. Sometimes they nickered plaintively or sniffed the ground as though hoping to pick up a scent of lost friends whose trails had long ago turned to dust.

South of my uncle's ranch the ponderosa forests gave way to broad lava tablelands bordered by rimrocks; here I could always find wild-horse tracks around the springs. Fascinated by the animals, I plotted to get another glimpse of them. I climbed the edge of the tableland, taking my time not to break a branch or scrape a limb. Often I surprised a big mule-deer buck in his bed, but when I peered over the edge of the table, across the vast flats of grasslands and fields of broken lava rocks, the horses were already running for the thickets a mile away. So many fresh tracks yet so few sighted horses.

The best way for me to see the wild horses was to hide out near water holes. That same summer when I was thirteen, I had just driven a small herd of cattle into some meadows southeast of the ranch, when I came upon the remnants of an old logging camp now grown up with jack pines. Years before, the loggers bulldozed out a spring and collecting pond, and there I watered my horse and untied my lunch from a salt sack tied behind my saddle. Tired from my long ride, I hobbled

my horse so he could graze. That accomplished, I lay down behind a log to nap.

I awoke to find my horse staring off across the pond at the jack-pine thickets, and, as I peered over the log, I saw movement among the trees. Wild horses were coming in to drink.

An old black mare was first. She took her time, advancing a few steps, then standing stock-still, staring at my saddle horse, and finally advancing a few more careful steps. Behind her in the forest, I glimpsed other horses standing quietly, waiting for her to determine if the place was safe. Once she snorted an alarm and retreated into the thickets, but soon she was back, moving forward a few feet at a time. A Steller's jay flew down to drink, and she watched it bathe, her conelike ears pricked forward, focusing as she thought about that bird. Impatient for water, a couple of thirsty yearlings tried to edge past her, but she laid back her ears to threaten them and they backed up.

At last the old black mare decided my horse posed no threat. She moved forward, wading knee-deep into the pond, submerging her lower jaw in water as she drank. I was so close I could see the muscles of her flank twitch to dislodge a deerfly. Two bay mares followed her, then came the two yearlings and a buckskin mare of incredible beauty. She had a jet black mane in which was tangled a bit of wolf moss, and her tail was a mess of cockleburs. Behind her came a strawberry-roan stallion, standing at the edge of the timber and watching the others drink. When the mares finished, they stood for a moment as water dripped from their chins, then backed up toward the shore as the stallion slipped past them to drink his fill.

The bay lead mare bit angrily at a horsefly on her hip, then lay down in the shallows to roll. Another mare pawed the spring with a jagged hoof, sending great gouts of water over the other horses. The buckskin mare bore the stub of a reata around her neck; it had worn a crease in her hide. She must have broken away from someone as they tried to rope her and had broken

A Dapple gray stallion at Carmody Lake, Wyoming.

the reata some sixteen inches from the honda, leaving just enough weight to keep the loop snug. The trailing end of the leather was frayed as though other horses had chewed on it.

The two yearlings reared and pawed each other in a mock battle. One fell sideways, bumping the old lead mare, who whirled in anger to bite the young animal and teach him some manners. The other yearling slipped away to avoid punishment and tried to nurse a bay mare who was evidently his mother. But the mare raised a back hoof as though kicking at a fly, and, thus warned, the youngster climbed a spoil bank to rub its nose on a branch.

I checked the horses over from my hiding place. There was not a brand in sight.

I could have stayed there watching for hours, but the stallion, after drinking, noticed my saddle horse and came trotting over to investigate. Afraid the stallion might attack my gelding, I stood up. Suddenly the whole herd, including the stud, exploded into action and charged off through the forest. My saddle horse made a couple of jumps toward them with front feet straining at his hobbles, and then stood staring at the forest where the wild horses had disappeared. A pall of volcanic pumice dust drifted off through the trees, and I could hear branches snapping as the wild horses fled down a ridge toward the Sycan River drainage.

There was silence then. I walked over to where the horses had been standing and looked at their fresh tracks in the mud. The hoofprints were there, and the clouded water still drifted out into the pond. I had tried so hard to see some wild horses up close, and having them run away from someone who intended them no harm didn't seem fair.

Throughout my young cowboying days I often frequented that magic glade and others, hoping for another look at that wild band, but I never saw them again.

In the winter, when the forests clogged with snow and the wild horses were winter-weak from eating frozen grass, the Indians rode out on grain-fed horses, picked up a trail of mustangs in the snow, and followed it. Their goal was to force the wild animals to break trail in the deep snows until they tired. Soon the riders came across piles of dung steaming in the cold. Then they could glimpse the rumps of the band ahead of them in the trees. Ropes down, they dashed into the midst of the band. One roped a colt by the neck while another roped its heels. As the colt crashed into the snow, a third rider dismounted and haltered the colt, anchoring a lead rope firmly to a tree. Then off the riders went until they caught up to the band again. When their day was over, they backtracked and led their captured animals to a home corral.

My favorite band of wild horses ran around Wildhorse Springs in southern Oregon. About a dozen grulla mares ran with a grulla stallion. The term "grulla" wasn't part of our vocabulary back then; we referred to them as the "blue velvet horses." They had black manes and tails and a black stripe down their backs. If one were lucky enough to capture foals from this band, they made great saddle horses. They were larger than most wild horses, probably weighing more than a thousand pounds. They ran in the Wildhorse Meadow country at the base of Fuego Mountain until around 1954, when they may have moved on or been captured. I never glimpsed them again.

One spring, I rode out into the Wildhorse country to determine how the wild horses had wintered. I found forty wild horses that had starved to death. (I was relieved, however, to find there were no grullas among them.) They had been trapped in chest-deep snow and eaten each other's manes and tails, as well as the bark from surrounding lodgepole pines. To this day I have the death of those horses on my conscience, for I might have saved them. For years after, I rode that country to make sure no other wild horses suffered such a cruel and unnecessary end. But I learned from the tragedy. When people talk of wild horses and how they should be allowed to fill up the empty spaces in the West, I feel a slow burn in my innards. I would rather see smaller

numbers of wild horses running on better ranges dedicated to them and well managed, so that the animals do not starve in a tough winter or die of thirst when water holes go dry.

Perhaps one of the finest saddle horses I ever encountered was a sabina gelding named Yamsi after our ranch on which he was born. When I was a boy, I never rode the horse, only watched him perform, for he was always the foreman's horse and no one else dared lay a hand on him. The boss rode him on cattle drives, separated cattle on him, roped on him, and dragged calves with him to the branding fire. He also entered Yamsi in local bridle contests and always won. It was not until I bought the cattle ranch from my uncle and became boss myself that I got the right to have the old horse in my string. When Yamsi died of old age in the 1960s, he was still the best horse I had ever been on.

When folks asked me Yamsi's history, I had to say I just didn't know much about him, other than he had been born on the ranch and that I would always remember him as the smartest horse I ever rode. He remained a mystery horse with no known mother or father.

Not long ago, I received a letter in the mail from the widow of an old cowboy who worked for my uncle a half century ago. In the letter were some faded photographs, including one of Yamsi as a foal nursing his mother. She was a fine mare owned by my uncle's partner, Margaret Biddle. On the back of the photograph, faded but legible, was written "Yamsi, out of the mare Nellie, by a wild stallion that jumped the corral fence."

I always wondered at the toughness of mustangs and their incredible endurance. North of our ranch, on a little creek called Deep Creek, lived our neighbor, an Indian lady named Mamie Farnsworth. Mamie ran cattle in the Deep Creek draws and well up the side of Yamsay Mountain. She also ran a band of perhaps forty horses, which she turned out after haying season to fend for themselves. Those horses mingled with the wild herds and always managed to drift back to the ranch with several mustang foals, which Mamie promptly branded with her AF brand.

Mamie was selling off some of her horses one day, and I climbed her corral fence to look them over. At the far edge of the herd stood a little brown gelding, as perfectly formed as any horse I had ever seen. The price was right, and I bought him for my uncle's ranch, where he was turned over to a cowboy named Slim Fields to break. I would have guessed the animal's age at about three, but Slim managed a look at the animal's teeth as

the horse put him over the corral fence and swore the gelding was at least six.

Slim Fields was a big man, weighing about two hundred and thirty pounds. The colt looked like a pony beside him, and we promptly called the horse Little Joe. With Slim's big saddle on his back, little of the horse stuck out at either end, and the other cowboys joked that Slim might end up climbing off and carrying the horse.

Slim rode the colt around the corral that evening and managed to get by without event. The next morning, however, as we headed north down the ranch to check cattle, Little Joe decided to buck as though it was the only gait he had. Slim rode him jump after jump and even managed to roll a Bull Durham cigarette while the little animal turned the crank. It was fifteen miles from the home corral to what was called the Lobert Field, and by the time we got there Little Joe still hadn't walked a step nor had he turned a hair with sweat.

And by now the aging cowboy was pretty well tired out.

"I could get off and walk back to the ranch," Slim said, "but my feet are killing me, and it would be a victory for the horse."

Slim ended up riding Little Joe into the Williamson River and riding him back to the ranch by keeping him in the middle of the stream. By the time we reached the ranch and left the river, the little mustang was still trying to buck. By our estimate the animal had bucked for thirty-five miles with no sign of ever wanting to quit. 🐎

BONDS BETWEEN MOTHERS AND FOALS
ARE CLOSE AND INVOLVE FREQUENT TOUCHING.
CUSTER NATIONAL FOREST, MONTANA.

WESTERN MUSTANGS SURVIVE IN COUNTRY WHERE FEW OTHER ANIMALS LIVE:
ON ARROWHEAD MOUNTAIN, MONTANA.

A HERD STALLION CHASES AN INTERLOPER AWAY FROM HIS HAREM
IN THE PRYOR MOUNTAINS, MONTANA.

HORSES ARE HERD ANIMALS AND RARELY FOUND ALONE; THIS LONE HORSE GRAZES
ON CROOKS MOUNTAIN, WYOMING.

WILD HORSES WALK INTO THE LAST LIGHT OF DAY
AT SANDWASH BASIN, COLORADO.

STALLIONS WORK TO KEEP THEIR HERDS SEPARATE AT A DESERT WATERHOLE
IN THE RED DESERT, WYOMING.

Top: A paint stallion drinks at leisure in the middle of a pond as others wait in the Red Desert, Wyoming.

Bottom: A stallion positions itself to stay between its harem and potential danger at a waterhole in the Red Desert, Wyoming.

Above: ALL OF TODAY'S WILD HORSES WERE ONCE
DOMESTICATED BEFORE BECOMING WILD AGAIN. DIVIDE BASIN, WYOMING.

Opposite page: ON ARROWHEAD MOUNTAIN, MONTANA,
BACHELOR STALLIONS SNORT, POSTURE, REAR,
AND KICK—ALL WITHOUT GETTING TOO AGGRESSIVE. THESE MOCK
BATTLES SERVE AS TRAINING FOR REAL BATTLES YET TO COME.
SUCH FIGHTS BETWEEN BACHELOR STALLIONS RARELY LEAVE SCARS,
AS THE BITES AND KICKS ARE NOT FULL FORCE.

In a year with good rain, grass is abundant and the horses thrive
at Carmody Lake, Wyoming.

A COLORFUL, WILD HERD UNDER THE FULL MOON
AT CARMODY LAKE, WYOMING.

Chapter 2

A SHORT HISTORY OF THE LONG TRAIL OF THE HORSE

PREHISTORY

WAY BACK IN TIME, when the vast continental plates were shifting like huge slabs of ice, breaking off into smaller units, bumping, grinding, mounting each other or breaking free, setting sail on unknown molten seas to cast permanent anchor thousands of miles from the land mass that gave them birth, a little three-toed animal the size of a modern fox lived in the forests of what is now North America. Solitary and elusive, it kept to the thickets of lush vegetation rather than chance being eaten by one of the hungry predatory reptilians that sought this primitive creature for food. This animal—which scientists now call Eohippus—was the progenitor of the horse.

In those ancient times, lightning fires burned unchecked. The fire served the developing grasses by building a prairie domain and keeping forests in their place. Higher, drier areas burned quickly and made a natural transition from slow-growth forests to open prairies. Little Eohippus likely made gradual grazing forays onto the endless sea of grass, exposing itself to predation. Those of the equine population who were larger, faster, more alert, and had keener eyesight survived being eaten. In time, the horse grew larger and moved to harder ground. Its toes were lost or moved up the leg, and the middle toe became a hard hoof, able to propel the animal over rocky terrain where few predators were equipped to pursue.

Perhaps two million years ago, through natural selection and survival of those most able to adjust to new conditions, the early horse became similar in size and form to the modern horse. An increase in size, stronger jaws, a back kick, and the ability to outrun its pursuers gave it a definite advantage over its ancestors. Both the abundance of grass and the animal's ability to handle coarser forages through a swift digestive system enabled it to survive even the leanest years. A heavy coat and the ability to traverse long distances in search of food helped it survive the challenges of the Ice Age, when glaciers covered much of North America.

The success of nutritious grasses and cereal plants in certain areas led to the proliferation of horses and other ungulates over eons of time, and they in turn furnished a huge source of protein for scavengers such as condors and predatory species such as cats, wolves, and bears.

The constant pressure of predation on the horse led it to develop its great speed, endurance, herd instinct, eyesight, and intelligence—a quality in the modern wild horse I like to refer to as "smarts." Likewise, the horse pushed the early development of its four-legged predators.

Horses also had a stake in shaping the development of humans; each had a part in changing the other's world. Early horses must have been a complete frustration to primitive man, for here was an animal that could outrun the wind, whose bands had sharp-eyed sentinels able to snort the herd into instant flight. It would have been impossible for a hunter to capture a healthy wild horse with his bare hands. Humans likely developed bows and arrows, spears, deadfalls, snares, and traps, as well as butchering tools such as stone knives and axes, to make themselves equal to other predators. As a principal predator, humans helped bolster the horse's success by making it fleeter of foot, more intelligent, and more alert, while the horse itself contributed greatly to man's hunting prowess, inventiveness, and athletic ability. Early primitives, however, lacked the imagination to see the horse as anything but a source of meat.

In ancient times, wild horses found safety in numbers, protecting themselves from predators by running in family groups bound together by strong emotional ties. Predators, having difficulty choosing between two animals, often pursue a group until the weakest one falls behind. It is easy to imagine a wild colt or filly, its companion falling to a wolf or lion, running off alone into strange territory and, desperate for companionship, wandering into a camp of early humans. If it were not immediately killed and eaten, the horse could have been kept as a camp pet or cherished as a hedge against a future food shortage. It would have been an important entry in the annals of mankind when someone discovered that the young animal had become tractable enough to do its share of moving camp as a beast of burden. But the greatest breakthrough was yet to come. Perhaps it was some daring child who crept up on the

animal's back and sat grinning down at his comrades, totally unaware of the future importance of the horse as a means of transportation or as a tool of war.

The sociability of the wild horse and its need for companionship could have contributed to the ease with which it was domesticated. Although the horse's ancestors originated in North America, domestication first occurred among nomadic tribes an ocean away, after wild horses migrated across land bridges to Asia and Europe. Harsh winters in England and the northern latitudes influenced the size and conformation of horses. The short-bodied, stocky, coarser equines needed less forage to survive the fierce winters, giving rise to English forest and moorland ponies such as the ancient Exmoor pony, one of the earliest of equids, and the small, stocky horses of Mongolia.

If there were any domesticated horses in the Americas at that time, the animals mysteriously vanished from the land at the close of the Pleistocene era about eleven thousand years ago. No one knows for sure what wiped out these populations. Stone age hunters were likely one factor in their disappearance. The southern movement of ice sheets could have driven horse populations farther south, making them even easier prey for human hunters. Another theory speculates the eruption of Mount Mazama in the Cascade Mountains could have darkened the sky and buried the food supply in volcanic ash, although the eruption could not account for deaths of animals beyond its lethal range. Humans survived that holocaust and moved fairly quickly back into the area, but it would be thousands of years before the thunder of horse's hooves was heard once more in the Americas.

Christopher Columbus brought horses back to the Americas when he landed at Hispaniola on his second voyage in 1493. But it was the later Spanish and Portuguese ships that imported large numbers of domesticated horses to be used in military conquest and in the exploration and exploitation of the continents for gold. Soon, in North and South America, horses were being bred in numbers to keep up with the demands of the church and military.

INDIANS AND WILD HORSES

The first sight of Spaniards mounted on horses must have struck terror into the hearts of Native Americans. They had never seen horses before and assumed the figures were half man, half animal; they were terrified, making their conquest easy. But early military successes caused the invaders to become complacent. Their horses had a way of escaping in the night and not all of them were recovered. During the exploration of what is now New Mexico, many more horses were lost and ended up running wild or in the hands of Indians. Stealing horses soon became a game. It was easy for the Indians to slip in under the cover of darkness and steal horses for their own use. As the years passed, they became an effective military outfit that exceeded the Spanish in horsemanship. As a mounted force, able to strike and vanish, they stole not only from the Spanish military, but also from other native tribes. Without horses of their own, these tribes were helpless against the raiding parties.

Before the advent of the horse, Indians were confined by distances to river valleys. Horses gave them mobility, enabling them to travel farther from water and to transport meat back to camp rather than having to consume game where it fell. Buffalo tended to be migratory and hard to kill, but the horse enabled the hunter to trail the herds for long distances, gallop alongside his running prey, and send arrows into vital parts.

To the Indian, the horse was regarded as a measure of wealth, and the more horses he could claim, the greater his status in the tribe. Along with blankets, beads, and articles of war, the horse became a principal item of exchange with which he could barter for rifles, ammunition, or even a new wife.

The spread of horses in the West did not happen overnight. It was a slow process that took almost three hundred years. The gradual acquisition of horses by native people slowed down the pace at which the West was settled. Superb natural horsemen, the Indians completely frustrated the efforts of the U.S. military to put them on reservations. The military attempted to control the native populations not only by killing off their most important source of food, the buffalo, but also by slaughtering thousands of their horses.

Indian management of horse herds was lax, and in time feral horses—descendents from the Spanish imports—and native herds filled every suitable niche and pushed north into Canada. By the late 1800s more than two million mustangs roamed the West. During that era of western expansion, it was horseflesh that plowed the virgin prairie grasslands, carried soldiers in pursuit of Indians reluctant to conform to their ways, powered a burgeoning cattle industry, and made the American cowboy a legendary figure.

There was a problem with the mustang, however: Even though its spirit and endurance were extraordinary, it wasn't big enough to do the jobs required of it. New stallions from coach and draft stock were introduced from Europe and bred to mustang mares, producing larger offspring more able to pack heavy roping saddles and portly cowboys. The pure Spanish or Portuguese bloodlines were soon polluted by a host of other breeds. But the pure mustang was able to survive in the wild, where many of the imports fell by the wayside before they had much influence beyond the first few generations.

In the ranch country of the West, horses were cheap. To avoid feeding animals during the wintertime, ranchers often turned out their saddle and draft horses to forage for themselves. These horses soon blended with wild stock so that, save for a few inaccessible herds in the back country, nothing was ever absolutely pure again.

Wild stallions, too, contributed to the loss of domestic stock to the wild. Bachelor stallions especially were adept at stealing domestic mares. Even when the

An Indian's wealth was measured by the horses he owned.

mares were tied to a fence or picket line, a stallion could move down the line, breaking lead ropes with his chest and freeing the tethered animals. Sometimes stallions busted the top logs of corrals by rearing up and letting the full weight of their bodies break down the barriers. Then it was an easy matter to drive the mares to freedom and make a disciplined band of them. A stallion intent on moving a reluctant mare, dropping his head and weaving snakelike, is impressive in his determination and fury, and mares seem resigned to yield to such a demonstration of force.

The development of the American West took a toll on the freedoms of Native American populations and the proliferation of wild horses. Indians were forced onto reservations, and wild horses were captured in large numbers. The advent of barbed wire made the gathering of wild horses commercially feasible, and soon the animals were slaughtered by the thousands for hides, pet and poultry food, and human consumption.

Long after Indian tribes were placed on reservations in the West, they retained their love of horses—even though possession of too many horses and too little grass had a hand in keeping them poor. Drive across any western state, even today, and you know you are on an Indian reservation when you see small ranches with far more horses than cattle. Over the years, wild and domestic horses continued to mix in the American West. Many of those Indian-owned herds roaming reservation lands took to the wild and, having escaped branding and castration, became indistinguishable from wild herds. ⚘

Above: HORSES HAVE AFFECTED MAN'S DESTINY MORE THAN ANY
OTHER ANIMAL. CUSTER NATIONAL FOREST, MONTANA.

Right: A WILD HORSE HERD GATHERS FOR SHADE IN THE MIDDLE OF THE DAY
UNDER THE ONLY TREE AROUND AT PRYOR MOUNTAINS, MONTANA.

Chapter 3

WILD HORSES OF THE WORLD

ZEBRAS

THERE ARE THREE species of zebra: the plains, the mountain, and the Grevy zebra, all confined to the African continent. Along with the modern-day mustang, they evolved from a common ancestor about two million years ago. Zebras are light-colored animals with black stripes, which help camouflage them in an arid land filled with predators. Slower than its cousin, the horse, the zebra relies on its stripes to conceal it and to confuse attacking predators. It also benefits from an evil disposition and a back kick that can break a lion's jaw.

The zebra fascinates students of the horse because its disposition has kept it from being domesticated. In the wild zebra we can observe traits that have not been altered by centuries of captivity, while the only horses left on planet Earth have been influenced by a period of domestication by man. By assessing the behavioral similarities between zebras and horses we can get a good idea of what their common ancestor might have been like. Sorraia mustangs exhibit certain traits of their ancestors, often showing remnants of zebra stripes on their legs and a dorsal stripe down their backs, as well as the dun coloration of early horses.

Sadly, there are probably no truly wild horses left anywhere on Earth, since the species has undergone centuries of genetic fiddling by humans. The wild horses that we love so dearly today are really feral horses, descendants of domesticated animals that have returned to the wild. Without the restraints of captivity, the feral horse gradually lost the influence of domestication and became wild once more. Scientists are too pure, too hard on the mustang; they infer that mustangs are of deteriorated or inferior stock, when in reality mustangs have qualities such as stamina and intelligence superior to other domesticated animals. We have only to look at the zebra to appreciate what wild traits the mustang has retained. The many behavioral and physical similarities between horses and zebras render that period of domestication in the history of the horse far less significant than one might think.

Both horses and plains zebras live in harems with one stallion who commands several mares. The mares and stallions resist newcomers and tend to keep strange mares from joining the band. Wild-horse harems disperse from other bands and scatter over arid lands; here, survival means constantly being on the move, because a sedentary life would soon abuse the land and its supply of grasses. The harem system thus gives the animals the skills to live in arid lands and wander about, although neither zebras nor horses can exist long without available water. In *The Behavior Guide to African Mammals,* Richard Despard Estes writes that the harem system is not that common in nature; it is limited to a few species of mammals, including gorillas, bush pigs, giant hogs, and hamadryas and gelada baboons, as well as zebras.

Courtship patterns of horses and zebras are almost identical, as are heat postures and mating actions. Common to both is the cooperative grooming of two equids—standing nose to tail, each animal swishes flies off the other or chews on the other's back or mane—

and the tendency of horses and zebras to travel in the company of other species, such as cattle or wildebeests. Both horse and zebra stallions mark territory by defecating in stud piles or urinating where a mare has gone. Horses and zebras also show the same techniques while fighting, dropping down low to protect their forelegs while grabbing at those of the rival stallion.

While zebras can be observed in their natural states, it is difficult to assess the effects of learned behavior on the habits of wild horses in North America. What, for instance, has been the influence of fences on their behavior? In the old days, wild horses might have had a greater tendency to migrate during the winter to ranges lower in elevation or farther south. Fences and highways have changed all that. My guess is that if captivity has had any effect on wild horses it has been to lessen the animal's instinct to seek out better ranges or water holes once theirs have been depleted. Love of a particular piece of range is strong in them. Run a bunch of horses away from their particular domain, and they will circle and be back where they started in the shortest possible time. If I had to design a more successful animal than the wild horse, I would increase its ability to adjust to change, to explore new areas and hunt for better sources of food and water.

Captive or wild, there are some equine instincts that will never change. With the arrival of spring, all horses have an instinct to return to the range or pasture where they were born or, in the case of certain mares, where they last bore young. On the cattle ranch where I grew up, we bought an occasional saddle horse that had been raised east of us on the Oregon desert. That animal was perfectly content until the following spring, when it might escape and head back to the desert where it had been born.

Above: ZEBRAS, LIKE WILD HORSES, STAND IN PAIRS
TO SWISH FLIES FROM EACH OTHER'S FACES AND TO SEE IN BOTH DIRECTIONS
AT THE ETOSHA NATIONAL PARK, NAMIBIA.

Opposite page: THE GREVY ZEBRA ARE THE LARGEST ZEBRA
AND THE ONLY TERRITORIAL ZEBRA.
THEY ALSO HAVE THE LONGEST GESTATION PERIOD OF ANY
EQUINE—THIRTEEN MONTHS. SAMBURU NATIONAL RESERVE, KENYA.

Above: THE GREVY ZEBRA ARE IDENTIFIED BY
THEIR CLOSE STRIPES AND LARGE ROUNDED EARS.
SAMBURU NATIONAL RESERVE, KENYA.

Right: PLAINS ZEBRA ARE ORGANIZED
IN BACHELOR GROUPS OR HAREMS WITH ONE
STALLION AND TWO TO FIVE
MARES THAT SOMETIMES SHARE A WATERHOLE.
ETOSHA NATIONAL PARK, NAMIBIA.

Although a zebra is capable of breaking a lion's
jaw with a good kick, their instinct is to run from danger.
Etosha National Park and Andoni Plain, Namibia.

FIGHTING BETWEEN STALLIONS CONSISTS OF BITING, REARING, AND KICKING, AND CAN RESULT IN SERIOUS INJURIES FROM TEETH AND HOOVES. ETOSHA NATIONAL PARK AND ANDONI PLAIN, NAMIBIA.

ZEBRA ARE MOST VULNERABLE WHEN DRINKING,
SO THEY REMAIN ALERT AND WATCHFUL AS THEY DRINK
AT ETOSHA NATIONAL PARK, NAMIBIA.

ZEBRAS ARE VOCAL WITH SEVERAL DIFFERENT CALLS.
THE PLAINS ZEBRA GIVES A CONTACT CALL THAT HAS A BARKING SOUND.
CHOBE PARK, BOTSWANA.

Fights are common near waterholes where Hartmann's Mountain
Zebra herds meet. These stallions fight after rolling in mud at the waterhole
at Etosha National Park, Namibia.

A Hartmann's Mountain Zebra stands
in a meadow of wild flowers during the rainy season
at Etosha National Park, Namibia.

HARTMANN'S MOUNTAIN ZEBRA HAVE ADAPTED TO THE
DUST AND WIND OF THE NAMIBIAN DESERT.

THE SURVIVING
STOCK OF ENDANGERED
GREVY ZEBRA IS
DOWN TO JUST A FEW
THOUSAND, ALL
IN NORTHERN KENYA.
LEWA DOWN, KENYA.

THE SOMALI WILD ASS IS NATIVE
TO THE DESERTS, BUSHLANDS, AND GRASSLANDS
OF NORTHEASTERN SOMALIA AND NORTHERN
ETHIOPIA. ALL MODERN DOMESTIC
DONKEYS—THE FIRST BEASTS OF BURDEN—ARE
DESCENDED FROM AFRICAN WILD ASSES.

WILD HORSES
OF THE NAMIB DESERT

No one knows for sure the origin of the wild horses that roam the desert of southwest Africa. They may be descendants of German cavalry horses left on the desert during World War I. These horses were able to adjust to Namibia's extremely harsh conditions and have managed to survive despite long journeys from food supply to water. In 1991 an aerial count put the population at 276 horses, but a devastating drought in 1992 was responsible for the death of thirty to forty horses. The population now stands at about 150.

In appearance, the horses of the Namib Desert look to be of Thoroughbred descent, but DNA studies show them to be closer to Arabians. They have developed an extra chromosome and are important for scientific studies, since it is doubtful that any new blood has reached them since they became feral around 1915. The animals are watched over by Namibia's government, which maintains a source of water for the animals at Garub. There, an observation post has been set up for tourists who come to view the horses.

Above: THE HARSHNESS OF THE LAND IN THE NAMIB DESERT HAS
THE ADVANTAGE OF A DRY CLIMATE THAT IS PARASITE FREE. AUS, NAMIBIA.

Opposite page: STALLIONS OFTEN FIGHT NEAR THE ONLY WATER IN THEIR
RANGE OF ABOUT 350 SQUARE MILES IN GARUB, NAMIBIA.

THE NAMIB HORSES
HAVE LIVED IN THE
AREA FOR
APPROXIMATELY A
CENTURY, PERHAPS
RUNNING WILD FROM
A GERMAN BARON'S
STABLE.
AUS, NAMIBIA.

BECAUSE OF THE
INHOSPITABLE
ENVIRONMENT AND
LACK OF WATER, THESE
NAMIBIAN HORSES
HAVE LEARNED TO GO
SEVERAL DAYS
WITHOUT DRINKING.
AUS, NAMIBIA.

The wild horses in the Namib Desert of Africa probably originated from German or South African army horses. Aus, Namibia.

IN THE FREQUENT DROUGHT YEARS, THE NAMIB HORSES
HAVE RESORTED TO EATING PODS FROM AN ACACIA TREE. GARUB, NAMIBIA.

A NAMIB HORSE DRINKS FROM DEPRESSIONS IN THE ROCKS
AFTER A RARE AUGUST RAIN IN AUS, NAMIBIA.

ONE THEORY ABOUT THESE HORSES' ORIGINS STATES THAT A SHIP
CARRYING THOROUGHBREDS FROM EUROPE TO AUSTRALIA RAN AGROUND
AND THE HORSES ESCAPED INTO THE DESERT. AUS, NAMIBIA.

THE NAMIB HORSES' HOME RANGE IS IN A RESTRICTED DIAMOND-MINING AREA,
FORBIDDING ACCESS TO POSSIBLE HORSE CATCHERS. AUS, NAMIBIA.

THE PRZEWALSKI HORSE IS THE ONLY TRUE WILD HORSE LEFT IN THE WORLD;
IT HAS BEEN CLASSIFIED AS EXTINCT.

PRZEWALSKI HORSES ARE BEING RE-INTRODUCED
ON THE STEPPES OF MONGOLIA FROM CAPTIVE ZOO STOCK.

THE SORRAIA WILD HORSE IS INDIGENOUS TO THE SOUTHERN IBERIAN PENINSULA.
IT IS AN IMPORTANT ANCESTOR OF MOST SPANISH HORSES.

SORRAIAS ARE ALWAYS DUN OR GRULLA IN COLOR WITH A DORSAL STRIPE;
THEY USUALLY HAVE ZEBRA MARKINGS ON THEIR LEGS AND WITHERS.

There were nine ancient breeds of ponies that developed in England.
The Exmoor pony is tough enough for the wet, windy, and cold winters
with a water-repellent, two-layer winter coat.

THESE PRIVATELY OWNED NEW FOREST PONIES ARE ALLOWED TO RUN FREE
IN THEIR ANCIENT HOMELANDS; THEY ARE ONLY ROUNDED UP IN THE AUTUMN.

DARTMOOR PONIES HAVE BEEN
ON THE MOORS OF ENGLAND FOR CENTURIES,
FIRST BEING MENTIONED IN THE
WILL OF A SAXON BISHOP IN THE YEAR 1012.

WILD HORSES OF
THE FRENCH CAMARGUE

In 1946, after the cessation of hostilities with Germany in the Second World War, I was bivouacked as an American GI near Arles, France, and got to know the delightful little wild horses of the Camargue well. To relieve the boredom of American troops awaiting shipment to the Japanese theater of war, as well as my own, I produced rodeos and bullfights every week in the great Roman coliseum in Arles.

We gathered black fighting bulls from the vast marshes of the Rhone Delta for the bull-riding events and used the Camargue horses for an event—if my memory serves me right—called *Cheval à Cheval*, in which a Polish expatriate named Godebski rode out bareback on a small Camargue horse and chased an unbroken horse round and round the arena until he was able to leap from his horse onto the back of the other. (Godebski and his wife were delightful people, and I regretted that language difficulties prevented me from learning more about his sport.)

As I remember, the little Camargue horses were rather rough gaited due to straight shoulders, but smoothed out considerably at a full gallop. They were of no use to me as bucking horses for they showed no inclination to buck. For the bronc-riding events I commandeered some large coach horses that had run out during the war and were captured for use in the rodeo. To bring bulls and horses from corrals deep in the Camargue marshes, we used special trucks with steel bars across the top, which prevented the animals from jumping out before we arrived at the coliseum.

The Camargue horses were specialists in saltwater living and waded about up to their knees in brackish water to forage. I was fortunate to meet a young horsewoman named Denise Puget, or "Poupette," whose family had vineyards on the delta and who drove me about in a wagon pulled by a team of white mules. Out in the marshes, amid reeds higher than our heads, we saw herds of white horses with little black foals. On occasion, in clearings, we would see herds of black, fighting cattle stock, which were raised for bullfights in the coliseums at Arles and Nimes.

The cattle and horses in the marshes seemed to spend much of their time trying to outwit the flies and mosquitoes, which followed us in clouds. The little horses would run to stay ahead of the clouds of tormentors, or roll and splash in the water and lie down until only their heads showed above the surface. They were a gentle lot, and we frequently had to stop the wagon to wait for them to get out of the way. I had expected them to be as wild as the horses I knew in my boyhood in Oregon and was a little disappointed when I found some of them delighted in being scratched.

Those little horses still exist in numbers in the Camargue, ridden by cowboys gathering cattle from the marshes, and their origin remains shrouded in mystery. From time to time, new blood has been introduced to the Camargue from other sources, but, as with our North American mustangs, this alien blood soon disappears, and the land, with all its unique hardships, builds the horse back to something of its original form. Camargue horses are of special interest since they represent some of the oldest equine blood on the planet and are close in form to the horses depicted in France's ancient Lascaux cave paintings, which are thought to be over ten thousand years old.

LIVING IN MARSHLANDS NEXT TO THE MEDITERRANEAN, THE
FRENCH CAMARGUE HORSES ARE OFTEN CALLED "HORSES OF THE SEA."

THE CAMARGUE HERDS ARE NO LONGER WILD, AS THE HORSES
AND THE LAND THEY RUN ON ARE NOW PRIVATELY OWNED.

THE CAMARGUE HORSE IS BELIEVED
TO BE DESCENDED FROM PREHISTORIC STOCK.

LIVING WITH FLOODED FIELDS IN MARSHLANDS, THE CAMARGUE HORSES OFTEN GRAZE
UNDERWATER FOR THE DELICATE NEW GROWTH. THE HORSES LOVE
AQUATIC PLANTS, PREFERRING FRESHWATER PLANTS OVER THOSE THAT GROW IN BRACKISH WATER.

NAPOLEON BONAPARTE SOUGHT OUT THE COURAGEOUS
CAMARGUE WILD HORSES FOR HIS ARMY.

THE CAMARGUE HORSES ARE UNFAZED BY THE FIERCE MISTRAL WINDS,
WHICH CAN BLOW FOR DAYS AT A TIME. AS FAMOUS FRENCH POET FREDERIC MISTRAL
WROTE OF THE HORSES, "THEY ESCAPED NO DOUBT FROM NEPTUNE'S CHARIOT."

Opposite page: CAMARGUE HORSES ARE PLAGUED BY MOSQUITOES,
FLIES, AND TICKS DURING THE SUMMER.

Above: THE WORLD OVER, HORSES HAVE THE SAME
NEED FOR DETERMINING THE PECKING ORDER WITHIN THE HERD.

CAMARGUE FOALS ARE BORN DARK BROWN, RUSSET, OR BLACK.
THEY GRADUALLY TURN WHITE BY AGE FOUR OR FIVE.

CAMARGUE HORSES HAVE LARGE HOOVES, IDEAL FOR NAVIGATING
THE MARSHLANDS. THE FOALS' SMALLER HOOVES OFTEN SINK INTO THE MUD
AND BECOME MIRED DOWN.

Food in the Camargue marshlands is not nutritious,
so the horses eat for fourteen to fifteen hours a day.

LIFE IN THIS HOSTILE, MARSHY AREA WITH POOR VEGETATION
HAS MADE THE CAMARGUE HORSES SMALL AND TOUGH. THEY ARE KNOWN
FOR THEIR ENDURANCE AND COURAGE.

ICELANDIC PONIES ARE DESCENDED FROM ANCIENT STOCK
BROUGHT TO ICELAND IN THE NINTH CENTURY BY THE VIKINGS.

THESE ICELANDIC PONIES HAVE AN EXTRA GAIT: THE TOLT,
A SINGLE FOOT FOR RUNNING WALK.

SORRAIA MUSTANGS

On the Black Hills Wild Horse Sanctuary in South Dakota is a herd of Sorraia mustangs that are registered and kept separate from the other wild horses. Despite the fact that the stallion is a bright bay, these animals are almost all bright bays, with black stripes down their backs, black manes and tails, and often with black tiger stripes or bracelets on their legs above the knees. Their heads are uniformly convex with the outwardly curved face of the original Spanish imports to the Americas. Their tail sets are rather low, and their inner ear cones are covered with dense hair.

The herd's uniform color and form speak to careful management of Sorraia bloodlines. These are beautiful little horses—gentle, quiet, and kind—probably more suited to pleasure riding than rough ranch work, although Sorraia fans have long touted the amazing stamina shown by the breed.

Most wild horses in the Americas show the genetic effects of crossbreeding. The original Spanish and Portuguese imports were small horses with prominent faces, not the dished faces of Arabians. Their tail sets tended to be low, and many were grullas and duns with black stripes down their backs, dark bracelets around their legs, and black manes and tails. They were tough horses by any standard, able to come off a voyage across the ocean and carry a Spanish soldier into battle or on a journey of exploration. It is doubtful that even these horses were pure Spanish since, in those days, there was considerable interest in crossbreeding to produce a variety of horse types for a variety of uses. Prominent in the genetic mix were the wild horses of the Iberian Peninsula, thought to be the main ancestors of the popular Andalusians and Lusitanos.

During the early eighteen hundreds, wild horses were common on North America's western prairies, and there was not much call for unbroken animals except for meat and hides. Cattle, chiefly of the longhorn breed, also ran wild, and soon a whole new professional

arose: the roper who could bring in wild cattle. Capturing a four- or five-year-old bull or steer required a larger horse, and inevitably crosses were made to increase the size and strength of the original mustangs.

War contributed to the further bastardization of mustang blood. Needing a ready source of horses for battle, the U.S. cavalry turned loose a host of fine remount stallions to cross with wild mares. The long-bodied thoroughbreds required far more food to feed their furnaces in winter, and the influence of their genes soon died out. Those that survived in the genetic pool were the stout, short-bodied types with incredible stamina. In any mustang herd today, no matter how polluted the blood, there is a constant return to form. It is the land that in the end shapes the wild horse.

Despite a near-constant pollution of wild-horse stock by other breeds, small islands of pure or nearly pure Spanish stock continued to exist. These stocks were captured by people of foresight who formed registries, such as Montana rancher Robert Brislawn's Spanish Mustang Registry, with the goal of keeping the remaining stocks pure. Brislawn recognized the presence of pure blood in wild horses on Indian reservations and spent much of his lifetime attempting to preserve it. At the Black Hills sanctuary there are two small bands of pure stock, one of Sorraia mustangs and one of Spanish mustangs from the Brislawns herd. These horses are considered domesticated, even though their ancestors once ran wild.

PRYOR MOUNTAIN MUSTANGS

Running the border between Montana and Wyoming, the Pryor Mountain wild horses are well known and attract a great many visitors. They number about one hundred and thirty head and tend to run in very small stallion bands.

DNA tests have proven that the Pryor Mountain mustangs trace back to the original Spanish horses imported to North America four hundred years ago. While some of the Pryor horses show a Spanish influence, not all have the convex heads and low tail sets of Sorraia mustangs and old-time Iberian horses. Others seem to differ from Sorraia types in conformation, which may show some influence from other equine blood. Pryor Mountain mustangs come in a variety of colors, but bay predominates.

A measure of controversy exists over the management of the Pryor herd. Some attribute the low production of foals to depredation by mountain lions; others think that the herd needs to be outcrossed with new blood. There are often differing views surrounding the management of wild horses, but the Pryor Mountain mustangs are lucky to have the support of volunteers, visitors, and experts on their side.

KIGER MUSTANGS

One of the best-managed Bureau of Land Management wild-horse areas is near Burns, Oregon. There feral stocks were manipulated to favor the development of a wild herd of Kiger mustangs, which closely resemble the early mustangs of Spanish and Portuguese origin.

Kiger mustangs are dun horses with dark manes and tails, and a black dorsal or eel stripe from mane to tail. They are extremely popular with the public due to the beauty of their coat and the elegance of their bodies; their heads lack the coarseness of some wild horses, probably because of introduced blood. Kigers resemble Sorraia horses, and they are smaller and more refined in bone structure than many western mustangs. Public demand for surplus individuals is good, which helps ensure the program continues.

NOKOTA MUSTANGS

The western Dakota Indians obtained horses in the seventeenth century and moved onto the plains, becoming the Lakota tribe. They were buffalo hunters and needed horses of squarish build with powerful hindquarters, short bodies, heavy bones, and great intelligence. The Nokota horses were bred to meet these requirements.

As with other wild-horse populations, some crossbreeding took place to give the horses more size and speed. The Nokota were crossed with Thoroughbreds and Percherons and are thought to have inherited good qualities from both. Certainly they are as beautiful as any of the wild horses that exist today. The severity of North Dakota's winters no doubt helped standardize the outcrosses with racing and draft types, for the Nokota require far more food than the shorter-bodied, closer-coupled, hardy wild horses with which they bred. Fierce winters or a few dry summers can decimate wild-horse herds, and only those of a certain type survive.

By 1960, the Nokota mustangs, enclosed by the boundary fences of Theodore Roosevelt National Park, were the last wild horses to exist in North Dakota. According to some, those horses were descendants of Indian ponies confiscated from Sitting Bull. Larger and rangier than your typical plains mustang, the Nokota resemble the horses painted by artist Frederic Remington.

When the National Park Service, which oversees Theodore Roosevelt National Park, decided to remove all wild horses from the grounds where they had lived since the 1880s, some of the horses were acquired by Frank and Leo Kuntz, ranchers from Linton, North Dakota. The Kuntzes deserve credit for keeping the Nokota bloodlines alive.

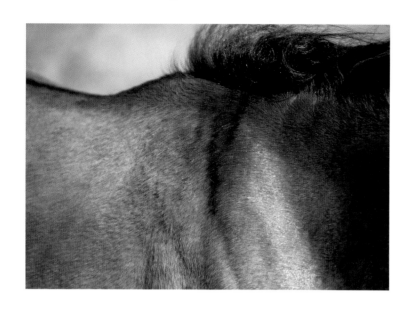

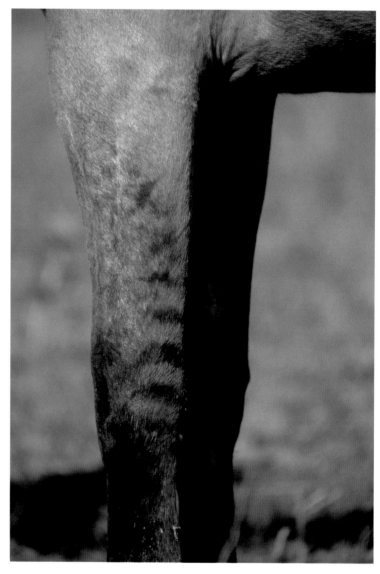

Zebra striping on legs
and withers are primitive markings
that show ancient bloodlines.
These markings are still common
in some Western herds
that have remained fairly pure.
Pryor Mountains, Montana.

A STALLION CURLS ITS LIP AS IT DETECTS THE SCENT OF AN ESTROUS FEMALE
IN THE PRYOR MOUNTAINS, MONTANA

KIGER MUSTANGS IN
OREGON HAVE
RETAINED THE LOOK
OF SPANISH HORSES
BROUGHT TO THE
WEST CENTURIES AGO.

WILD PONIES OF CHINCOTEAGUE AND ASSATEAGUE

In 1947, Marguerite Henry wrote the classic children's book *Misty of Chincoteague*, which made famous the ponies running wild on Assateague Island, a barrier island just off the Virginia and Maryland coasts. Overnight, Henry made every nine-year-old girl in America wish for a Chincoteague pony.

The origin of the famous ponies that run free on Assateague Island is shrouded in the mists of time. What is certain is that the ponies have lived on the island for over two hundred years. According to legend, the horses escaped from wrecked pirate ships. But more likely they originated from herds belonging to early Maryland and Virginia farmers, who pastured horses, sheep, and cattle on the islands, driving them from the mainland at low tide and gathering them after the pasture season.

Assateague Island lies in both Maryland and Virginia, and a fence separates the two territories. The wild horses on the Virginia end of the island are much less accessible to the public and are, therefore, much more timid. The Virginia horses are managed for the benefit of the Chincoteague Island fire department, which—after a series of disastrous fires in the 1920s that sapped their funds—began gathering the ponies on Assateague, swimming them across the half-mile channel to Chincoteague, and auctioning off the foals to help defray the department's fire-fighting expenses.

Through the years, the annual event has become one of the area's biggest tourist attractions. Thousands of people flock from all over the country to watch as local cowboys gather the wild ponies and swim them across the shallow channel. After a proper rest, the foals are separated from the mares and auctioned off to the highest bidders. Some are returned to the herd to maintain its numbers.

The foals are used to people and make good pets and riding horses for children. Because of the coarseness of their diet and the salinity of the water they drink, the Chincoteague ponies have rather large bellies. The addition of outside blood to the herd has added color. There are a number of paints, buckskins, and pintos. Those with the original brown and white colors of the famous Misty bring the most money at auction.

Tourists are also able to view the ponies in their natural habitat, although they are warned not to approach the animals too closely for safety reasons and to bring along lots of mosquito repellent. Feeding the horses is not allowed for it creates behavioral problems such as aggressiveness among the animals.

The ponies spend most of their time grazing or resting, perhaps because of the low nutritional value of the forage and the anemia produced by clouds of mosquitoes and hordes of biting flies. It is said that the animals rarely gallop until they are pursued by horsemen at the time of gathering. Much of the time, the ponies lead a lonely existence, pestered by insects in summer and by fierce Atlantic gales in the winter.

The wild horses of the East Coast barrier islands are important in their availability, for they are the only wild or feral horses most of the eastern public gets to see. Every year the thousands of faithful that attend the festivities and auction reinforce the horses' importance to the area, and owning a Chincoteague pony has become the dream of many a child. Those ponies carry a banner for wild horses everywhere, proving that wild horses can be a great drawing card and improve the tourism economy of any community lucky enough to have them as neighbors. ⚘

CHINCOTEAGUE PONIES WERE MADE FAMOUS BY
MARGUERITE HENRY'S 1947 BOOK *Misty of Chincoteague.*

WILD PONIES GRAZE IN THE SALTY MARSHES
OF ASSATEAGUE ISLAND, MARYLAND.

The "Saltwater Cowboys" of the Chincoteague
Volunteer Fire Department gather the ponies once a year
and drive them to corrals on the south end
of Assateague Island, Virginia. Most of the foals and yearlings
are auctioned off; the proceeds fund the fire department's
care of other ponies left on Assateague Island.

WHILE CORRALLED, THE PONIES ARE EXAMINED BY VETERINARIANS
BEFORE THE SWIM TO CHINCOTEAGUE ISLAND.

DRIVEN BY THE SALTWATER COWBOYS, THE PONIES MAKE A 100-YARD
SWIM DURING SLACK TIDE WHEN THE CURRENT IS STILL.
LESS THAT FIFTEEN MINUTES LATER, THE PONIES CALMLY COME ASHORE
ON CHINCOTEAGUE ISLAND TO GRAZE AND REST.

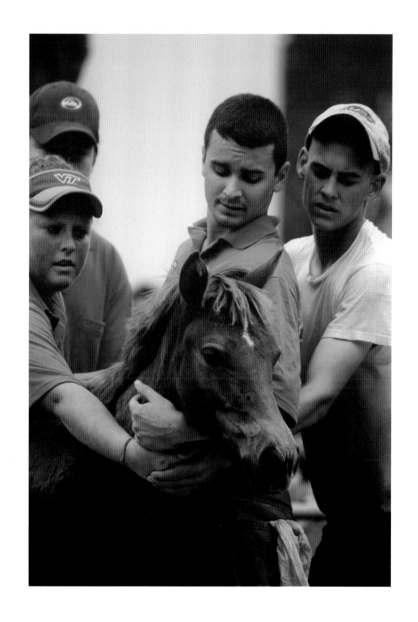

A FEW CHOICE FOALS ARE RETURNED
TO ASSATEAGUE ISLAND TO PRESERVE THE HERD.

THE PONIES ARE HERDED THROUGH STREETS LINED WITH SPECTATORS
TO BE PENNED AT THE CHINCOTEAGUE CARNIVAL GROUNDS.

PRICES PAID AT THE ANNUAL AUCTION KEEP SETTING RECORDS,
ESPECIALLY SINCE THE CHINCOTEAGUE PONY BECAME A REGISTERED BREED IN 1994.

WILD HORSES WALK THE OUTER BANKS OF NORTH CAROLINA
ON THE NORTH END OF COROLLA ISLAND.

Chapter 4

PROTECTING OUR WILD HORSES

HOME ON THE RANGE

BY 1930, most of the West had been broken up into private ranches, except for the land considered too unproductive for ranchers and farmers to pay taxes on. These lands, often interspersed with private holdings, ended up in the public domain. In many cases, private interests controlled vast areas of rangeland by controlling the water. Deer and elk passed through fences at will, but wild horses were forced into arid areas unable to support cattle and sheep. Often the horses traveled long distances to water and were unwelcome intruders on the better ranges, where they competed with livestock.

Driven by necessity, wild horses soon developed a bad reputation in the West. They sought relief from marauding insects by wading in water holes, pawing and splashing until the pond became a mud wallow. In the arid climate, destruction of precious water resources was not appreciated, and the horses made enemies when they could have used friends. In addition, wild horses had not the slightest sense of conscience, and many ranchers struggling for existence awoke in the morning to find their crops trampled and fields muddied by

nighttime visitors. The horses possessed an innate intelligence and would sometimes stand by as elk tore down stack yard fences, then invite themselves in to consume a rancher's precious stack of hay.

But for every rancher who hated wild horses there were many more that tolerated them or even loved them. Extremes of weather are a fact of life in the West, and many a rancher opened his gates to starving mustangs and over-wintered them from his precious supply of hay. Maybe it wasn't all kindness on the man's part, but chances were that he had grown up with wild horses as part of his life, valued them as something that might not be around forever, and realized how lonely the land would be without them.

One of the problems with wild horses is that they develop an extreme affection for their home territory. When persistent drought dries up the water sources, and grass withers and turns to dust, many animals perish rather than move to better ranges. In early times, predators such as wolves, bears, mountain lions, and mustangers harassed the herds, often driving them off to new ranges and breaking up family groups. Without predators, including the ranchers who chased them, horses have a tendency toward inbreeding.

Although a stallion will often drive off his daughters and his male offspring when they become interested in mares, the young, exiled males form stallion bands, and many of them are not lucky enough to acquire a harem of their own in their lifetime. On a range where several bands of mustangs compete, there is a constant shift of mares and fillies from one stallion harem to another. As much as a stallion would like to have more mares, he has a hard time keeping a harem larger than ten or fifteen together. From time to time, the mares make a game of escaping to be serviced by a rival stallion. Sometimes on realizing that a favorite mare is missing, a stallion will leave his band and, pausing now and again to sniff the ground, trail the escapee for miles, cut her from the rival's band, and run her unceremoniously back into his harem.

On ranges where there is little competition or disturbance, a stallion's harem might consist of a great-grandmother, grandmother, mother, and a few daughters, all related to the stallion. This situation unfortunately is all too common and cannot promote genetic health in a herd. Indians understood this and put new blood into the bands. Ranchers also understood this from their experience with livestock, knew the importance of mixing new genes to produce hybrid vigor, and often replaced wild stallions with their own. It has been said that the mustang shaped the West, but the real horses that shaped the territory were probably hybrids, an outcrossing of wiry, resilient, smart little mustang mares with domestic stallions. Many ranchers had a stake in the welfare of wild horses, for these horses belonged to no one and were a great asset to the rancher who needed a source of good saddle animals. Capturing wild horses became a sport and part of growing up for many a ranch boy and girl, who used the animals to ride to school. Over time, horse traders, cowboys, and ranchers played a large part in thinning the number of wild horses who roamed the prairie. Much has been written about cruelties imposed on wild horses by those who captured or attempted to capture

them. Unfortunately, there is no totally foolproof and humane system for catching them, regardless of whether it is done by individuals or by trained government personnel. The horses have spent their lives in the wild avoiding danger by taking to their heels in group panic and escaping by fleetness as well as intelligence. They will try to escape until no try is left in their bodies, and however padded and secure the holding corral, some animals will find a way to hurt themselves. They are, after all, wild animals forced into a new and frightening situation and faced with a predator that has been an enemy since birth. After living among friends, generally in a family situation, the captives often find themselves among strange horses where the old order no longer exists.

Generally, panic in a few horses will set off a chain reaction of panic in the whole herd. Even on the range, the sight of a band of horses running in the distance for whatever reason—fear or merely exuberance—will set off a fear reaction in neighboring bands. These bands are generally led by older, wiser mares; the stallions follow behind to protect the harem since experience has taught them that danger generally comes from the rear. If danger persists, bands often join together as individuals seek anonymity in the larger herd. Some cagey old lead mares, however, will split from the main bunch and take their followers down a tried-and-true escape route that may have led them to safety on past occasions.

The ploys used by lead mares to escape are legendary. I have seen them lead their band full tilt toward a fence or barrier, then suddenly skid to a stop while the rest plow through the barricade and open up an escape route. Lead mares know every break in the rimrocks, every trail to safety. Once they are driven to an unfamiliar range, they are far easier to handle. Any herd of horses is a mixture of animals in prime condition and old, partly crippled individuals, pregnant mares, and young foals that have difficulty keeping up with their mothers over long distances. Some of those individuals are lost in the gather, and they wander the ranges alone and vulnerable to predation until accepted into another band.

Perhaps the most efficient, albeit the most expensive, method of gathering wild horses is by helicopter. Skilled pilots maneuver fleeing bands of mustangs toward camouflaged corrals, where hidden riders emerge from cover to complete the capture. All manner of wings are built onto the corrals to lead the animals into them.

In the days before airplanes, some old-time horse runners plowed a V-shaped rut across the vast grasslands of the prairies. The horses followed the shallow ditches, afraid to jump across, until they were suddenly trapped by stout fences leading to log corrals, from which there was no escape.

Perhaps the gentlest method of capture is to trap wild horses around familiar water holes, using fences to lead them into stout corrals. Horses must have water, and thirst often overcomes the fear of their surroundings. This method is of little use, however, where water is plentiful; and, as humane as the trapping method may be, the wild horses inevitably panic when the trap is sprung and the gates are closed on their freedom.

THE WILD HORSE AND BURRO PROTECTION ACT OF 1971

People who love wild horses became a political force in the late 1960s. As the story goes, a Nevada secretary named Velma Johnston was waiting in her car at an intersection behind a livestock truck loaded with horses heading for slaughter, when she noticed blood dripping from the truck. Velma was shocked by the mistreatment of these animals. The woman, who became known to friend and foe alike as "Wild Horse Annie," organized a massive letter-writing campaign by schoolchildren, which was instrumental in convincing Congress to pass an act that would protect wild horses and burros.

Crippled by polio, Wild Horse Annie was physically weak, but she had an inner strength that carried her through her crusade. The Wild Free-Roaming Horses and Burros Act was passed in 1971, and Congress gave the management of wild horses and burros to the Bureau of Land Management.

Not everyone was thrilled by Wild Horse Annie's bill. A great many ranchers owned horses that had been turned out or escaped to public ranges, and those ranchers were given a limited amount of time to gather and reclaim their property. Sportsmen worried that wild horses would have an adverse effect on wildlife, and cattlemen worried that wild horses would increase in numbers and become a nuisance both on public ranges and on adjoining or interspersed private lands. Some land managers had wild horses shot because they feared wild-horse management areas would be set up on their home turf.

Even among those of us who loved wild horses, there was disagreement as to the long-term effects of the act. In certain remote areas of the West, there were still pockets of wild horses that closely resembled those brought to the Americas by the Spanish. Because of the act, the fifteen thousand or so horses still on the range would lose their last predator: man. Since wild-horse bands left to themselves grow at a rate of fifteen to twenty percent a year, many of us feared a population explosion of feral horses and escaped ranch horses that would genetically overpower the precious remnants of Spanish blood.

I was a rancher in Oregon in 1970, living on a remote ranch in the south-central section of the state, surrounded by wild horses, when I was asked to speak to a convention of humane societies and wild-horse groups in Chicago. I had never met Wild Horse Annie, but knew of her. In my address I talked about how the wild-horse protection act would remove the last predator left to mustangs and that any population without a predator would suffer a population explosion, as well as other deleterious effects. After my speech, a woman rushed up to the podium and gave me a big hug and kiss on the cheek. It was Wild Horse Annie. I had a feeling that I had poured my heart out, but she hadn't listened to any views she didn't want to hear.

The act proved a nightmare for the Bureau of Land Management to administer. Wild-horse populations increased from perhaps fifteen thousand animals to sixty thousand animals, necessitating frequent gathers of surplus animals and an adoption program that works hard to find homes for the fanciest of them.

A hierarchy soon built up around the Bureau of Land Management program. There are wild-horse experts, range managers, equine veterinarians, wild-horse clinicians, capture personnel, adoption experts, and birth-control researchers. The program now requires a forty-million-dollar-a-year federal budget, and many of us question whether some of those who make their living from wild-horse related activities really want a logical solution to the problem of wild-horse surpluses.

Unfortunately for the wild horses, any attempt by the Bureau of Land Management to cut down the herds to sensible levels has been met by public outcry from good, caring folks who think that this will lead to the demise of the wild horse. These fears are fueled by organizations that have found a lucrative source of funding by working the wild-horse issue for all that it is worth. Forget emotion. What is needed is a tough but logical program consistent with good biology and range management. In the end, it will be best for the health and future of the horses if those who contribute to management decisions come to understand all sides of the overpopulation issue.

WHERE WILD HORSES RUN FREE

My first attempt to protect a herd of wild horses was almost an accident. It was 1970, just before the Wild Free-Roaming Horses and Burros Act was slated to take effect, and I was upset that people were capturing or shooting wild horses all over the West, hoping to rid

their ranges of the animals before the congressional act became valid.

Back in the 1930s, my uncle had bought a tract of land halfway to the railroad town of Chiloquin, as a way station where he could rest his cattle as he drove them to the railroad stockyards for shipment. Beyond a water source and some meadows, with a rickety corral and loading chute, there was not much here. The lower field, however, was surrounded by some pretty good fence with a gate on the southern end that opened onto national forest lands. Often I found wild-horse tracks on the mountain above the field. When I became worried about the welfare of those horses and afraid they would be shot, I opened the far gate and scattered a truckload of hay on the snow. A week later, I was headed to town for a funeral, dressed in my Sunday best, when I looked down across the field and saw a herd of wild horses feeding on the hay.

Parking my car, I made a wide circle through the pine woods and closed the gate just as the animals sensed my presence and attempted to escape. Now at least I had the animals trapped on my private land, and no one could bother them without trespassing. But I knew that I would have to figure out a way to capture the horses and move them to sanctuary on the main ranch where I could better protect them.

I talked a friend into helping me. We unloaded our horses from a truck parked at the loading chute and propped up, as best we could, the flimsy corrals. Once the horses saw us, of course, they thundered off through a dust of fresh snow and disappeared into the trees at the lower end of the field. Clearly we would have to tire them out before they could be handled.

The field was a long rectangle, and my friend and I kept the horses between us as they ran back and forth in the light snow. I began to realize the power and speed of these animals as they tried to escape and knew that even if we managed to corral them, those flimsy panels would be no match for their terror. Once they knocked down the fence, they would be back on national forest

ONCE CORRALLED, CLOSE INSPECTION
SHOWS THE MAJESTIC BEAUTY OF A
WILD STALLION, SALT WELLS CREEK, WYOMING.

lands, where they would eventually be hunted down and shot. I was making one last attempt to move the horses toward the corral when they began jumping fences. The more they jumped, the more they ended up toward the center of the corrals. Suddenly they were beside the chute and, attempting to escape this predicament, thundered up the loading chute into the empty truck. I leaped over my horse's ears, jumped several fences, and as the last horse gained entry I slammed the door shut. In the truck were eighteen head of wild horses that would never be harassed again.

I had countless experiences over the years that strengthened my connection to wild horses, and in 1987 I embarked on an adventure that was to consume my life: I was bound and determined to set up a sanctuary for wild horses that would allow them to run wild and free.

I did not see sanctuaries as a solution to the problems of wild-horse management, but as an immediate means to get thousands of unwanted, unadoptable wild horses out of government holding facilities, which were often crowded and miserable. I was practical enough to know that even though I was short on money, I needed to purchase thousands of acres of grasslands, well watered and tightly fenced to contain mustangs. This

had to be accomplished before I set off for Washington, D.C. to persuade Congress and the head of the Bureau of Land Management that I was a man who could get the job done without bringing embarrassment to the Reagan administration.

In 1988, I was negotiating for three large ranches in the Flint Hills of Oklahoma when the governor of South Dakota, George Michelson, offered to fly me over a large piece of land in the Black Hills. Originally purchased by the Honeywell Corporation as a weapons testing area, the land had since been donated to the South Dakota Community Foundation in the face of public pressure. Much of it was short-grass prairie, and the cattle and horses in the area possessed an extraordinary shine of good health to their coats. The land contained several miles of the Cheyenne River and was potentially the best horse range in the country. Tourism had to support a sanctuary operation, and the land's proximity to Mount Rushmore and other Black Hills attractions gave me dreams of success. I had every hope that the public would enjoy seeing herds of wild horses running free on thousands of acres of some of the most dramatic scenery in the West.

It took six months in Washington, D.C. to convince Congress and the Bureau of Land Management that an old cowboy's dream could work. Finally, it happened.

WHEN WILD HORSES RUN FROM DANGER, THEY ARE LED BY THE DOMINANT FEMALE WITH THE HERD STALLION BRINGING UP THE REAR. BITTER CREEK, WYOMING.

Three hundred wild mares were trucked from holding facilities in Bloomfield, Nebraska, and turned loose on the Black Hills Wild Horse Sanctuary.

After nearly twenty years, we are still here. The sanctuary has provided over ten thousand horse-years of freedom to unwanted wild horses, and last year over twenty thousand tourists came to see the animals. Tourism dollars, money earned from the sale of foals, and gifts to our nonprofit outfit from caring individuals have helped us struggle through some lean years. Volunteers keep us going. The manager, Susan Watt, saw the sanctuary featured on ABC's news program *20/20* and has now volunteered here for ten years. I have volunteered since the sanctuary's inception. Our staff of hard-working horse lovers, from far and wide, makes it possible to spend donations where they should be spent, not for salaries but for the welfare of the animals.

The sanctuary is an oasis for wild horses, providing them with ample room to run, food to eat, and water to drink. Many people underestimate wild horses' need for water and can't understand why all the vast plains and mountain ranges of the West can't be a home for wild horses and buffalo. Although they can travel longer distances to water than cattle, wild horses and buffalo will soon die without a source of water. Most areas in the West that possess good water supplies are already settled and overrun with humans, or the drinking areas are fenced.

I have seen horses paw and roll until their favorite drinking hole is mud, yet they seem unwilling to leave that once magic spot to look for water elsewhere. On occasion wild horses have been transported to a new range well watered by an accessible river only a little distance away, yet have refused to leave the area where they were turned loose and died of thirst.

When horses first came to the Black Hills sanctuary, we unloaded them from Bureau of Land Management trucks into a corral with a huge tank of drinking water and kept them in that corral until every one of them was comfortable with the water source. Only then did we turn them out into an adjoining training field surrounded by well-marked and ribboned barbed-wire fences so they could learn barbed wire. I dwelt among them, sleeping and eating in the seat of my truck, until they were used to the sight of me and my pickup. I worried that they were not going to go back down that hill to drink, but every morning there were fresh horse tracks on the hill and signs that they had gone back into the corral to the water tank.

One moonlit night, I sat up and watched for the horses to drink. Hours passed. At about two o'clock in the morning, I saw white faces as the horses came tiptoeing down the hill toward the water. They moved silently, pausing to sniff the air for danger and look for predators waiting for them by the watering place. Once they had watered, they charged out of the corral with a clatter and didn't stop running until they had reached a comfort zone high on the hill. Some minutes later another band came in silently, drank, and clattered out of there. At times a small band would slip down the hill just as the others went charging up. Invariably, the newcomers would turn and flee with the others, only to slip down again a few minutes later to drink their fill. Worried as the horses were about danger and entering that hated corral, they had to come. It was drink or die, and a thirst for water overcame their fears.

I had learned a valuable lesson about water and wild horses at my ranch in Oregon, where vast areas east of the ranch possessed not even a seep spring. One day as I was patrolling the cattle with an old cowboy, four wild horses came down out of the arid eastern land and stood eyeing the fenced-in water of the Williamson River. There was a gate there, and the old cowboy was all for letting in the wild horses.

"They're pretty well ganted up," I said. "I'll go back to the ranch and get some buckets so they can have a little water at a time."

I returned just fifteen minutes later, but the old cowboy had felt so sorry for the animals he had opened the gate. All four animals gorged themselves on water, took their last drink, and lay dead along the river. The buckets could have limited their intake and saved their lives. It was one of many lessons I have learned about wild horses and used in our efforts at the Black Hills Wild Horse Sanctuary.

Recently, the Wild Free-Roaming Horse and Burro Act of 1971 was modified by the Burns Amendment, which gave the Bureau of Land Management the option to dispose of captured wild horses over nine years old that had been through the adoption program without

finding homes. Fifty-two of those animals ended up on the Rosebud Indian Reservation in South Dakota and were eventually sent to Illinois for slaughter.

Alerted by actress Stephanie Powers, the Ford Motor Company intervened, buying the animals from the dealer and sending them to our Black Hills sanctuary. The animals ranged in age from nine to twenty-five and were in reasonable condition, considering all they had been through.

After a few days of quarantine with good food and water, the animals were released to sanctuary ranges. They burst from the corrals like children at recess but skidded to a stop when they saw grass. They kept their heads down, grazing as though they feared the open gate had been a mistake and soon someone would come along to drive them back into the corral. Many of them were stallions that had been recently gelded, and a few had yet to realize they were no longer capable of breeding.

Although the geldings do not show interest in mares, they still defecate in stud piles, some of which are three feet high. That old habit of stallions apparently dies hard. Fighting amongst the new group has died down since the mares wandered up into the hills and found their own little piece of range with good water and grass. There has been little attempt by the new mares to join existing herds, although some of the geldings have moved back into the high country and joined harems led by stallions, apparently without incident.

These new horses will never be shipped off again, but will live out their remaining years in freedom.

Mustangs are rounded up by a Bureau of Land Management helicopter in the Lander Herd Management Area, Wyoming.

A helicopter pilot coaxes in a stray horse that could not keep up with the herd in the Lander Herd Management Area, Wyoming.

On a BLM round-up, cowboys on horseback
take over from the helicopter for the last few hundred yards
into the corral at Conant Creek, Wyoming.

A COWBOY WITH
A PLASTIC BAG FLAPPING
ON A FLEXIBLE STICK
MOVES THE CAPTURED
HORSES THROUGH
THE CHUTES AT BUFFALO
CREEK, WYOMING.

A PAINT STALLION
CONFINED FOR
THE FIRST TIME IN HIS
LIFE, BUFFALO CREEK,
WYOMING.

Above: WILD HORSES CORRALLED FOR POTENTIAL ADOPTION.
ADOPTION SALES PLACE MANY
WILD HORSES WITH LOVING OWNERS. LANDER, WYOMING.

Opposite page: STALLIONS ARE SOMETIMES FRANTIC WHEN CONFINED FOR THE FIRST
TIME AND OCCASIONALLY WILL BE SUCCESSFUL IN ESCAPING
STOCK CORRALS AFTER A ROUND-UP AT SALTS WELLS CREEK, WYOMING.

WIND COMBS THE MANES OF THREE PAINTS RUNNING ACROSS THE SAGEBRUSH PRAIRIE
AT CONANT CREEK, WYOMING.

DUE TO THE WILD HORSE ACT OF 1971, THESE SYMBOLS
OF THE WILD WEST WILL CONTINUE TO INHABIT WESTERN LANDSCAPES.
BEAVER RIM, WYOMING.

This dapple gray's long tail is ideal for keeping flies
off its hindquarters, Carmody Lake, Wyoming.

Mustangs' small, strong hooves are perfect for standing up
to the rigors of the difficult terrain at Cyclone Rim, Wyoming.

Chapter 5

SEASONS ON THE WILD HORSE SANCTUARY

From the bunkhouse door, the old cowboy, Slim, moves out for a moment into the darkness, stares uneasily at the starless murk above him, bunches his collar close about his neck with a forward roll of his shoulders against the maddening wetness of the flakes, kicks down with one pointed toe of a boot through the snowy carpet for one last reassuring look at the dirt before Spring, then heads back indoors, filled with a melancholy he cannot understand to smoke the last cigarette of the day in the comfortable overheat of the ticking wood stove.

—Dayton O. Hyde, *Yamsi*, 1971

WINTER

MORE THAN THIRTY YEARS have passed since I wrote those lines, but my dread of winter still exists. Not so much, I suppose, because of the sheer discomfort of facing the hurt of wind chill on my cheekbones, but because with winter comes responsibility for the wild horses that are my family. With every passing day the hay pile becomes smaller and spring seems farther away.

The wild horses on the Black Hills sanctuary appear to enjoy the snow, taking great gulps from the drifts even when open water is available. Their coats are thick, so well insulated, in fact, that snow clings to their bodies without melting. Chunks of ice rattle on their fetlocks as they walk, and their iced-up tails can be tools of destruction.

Winter is a time to save energy, and the wild horses make no moves that are not necessary to their survival.

There will be time enough to gallop and frolic when spring brings the greening of the ranges.

Wind sweeps the ridges clean, piling the snow in canyons, making canyon travel impossible until spring. Under the snows, the short prairie grasses are brown and sere. The horses paw the snow or graze in the tracks of a horse that has gone before. Those short grasses that appear so devoid of food value are more nutritious than they look. The horses winter well on them and will stay in good condition until the first blackroot or curly buffalo grass springs from the sandy hillsides.

From my window in the 1887 prairie house, I can look across the Cheyenne River at rocky hillsides that are nearly always bare of snow and are favorites of several groups of wild horses. Here in the early morning cold, sheltered from west winds, they turn broadside to the sun, exposing as much surface as possible to its rays

A MUSTANG WITH ITS WHISKERS COATED IN ICE
FROM PUSHING THROUGH SNOW TO FEED.

for warmth. Motionless against the vastness of the hillsides, they are hard to see until one switches its tail in anger, or jockeys for a better position in the sunshine.

Through the years I have come to know those side-hill groups well. But this winter there are more horses than usual. Last fall, a forest fire burned over a thousand acres of sanctuary land. For a week, the skies were full of helicopters, which frightened the horses and caused them to first bunch up in terror on the meadows, then depart in the night for other parts of the sanctuary. They have yet to return to their old haunts.

Snow on snow. The night wind mutters around the eaves of the old prairie house. Sometimes in the morning when I look out to see what the night has brought, I see groups of wild horses grazing on the meadow. They love to roll in the fluff of new snow, making horse angels in the pristine white. They look up as I call to them, and then go on grazing, pawing down to the remnant grasses of summer. Their hoofbeats are muffled by the snow, and they move slowly, saving their strength. They avoid steep hillsides these winter

days, where a slip on hidden ice might send them tobogganing down the steeps to their deaths.

Before I put new siding on the windward side of the house, replacing the old clapboards that had been cut to lacework by sands flung by persistent winter winds, I didn't have much chance to be lonely, for a host of voices spoke to me from the cold darkness outside. I never recognized their language, never knew whether they told me stories or only chatted about the unknown lands that birthed the winds that carried them here. Often I lay in bed listening intently for just one word that might betray the origin of the voices, but it was as unrewarding as listening for messages from outer space. Down deep, I knew it was only the prairie winds playing their mischief with me, as though I were meant to hear but not to understand.

Whatever acoustical changes I made by tacking on new lumber may have offended them, for their dialogue ended. I was left with sounds I could comprehend and images that were part of my everyday life on the sanctuary.

WILD HORSES GO
INTO WINTER IN
GOOD CONDITION
AFTER FEEDING
ON SUMMER GRASSES.

One cold winter night I bundled up in a heavy coat and left the comfort of the prairie house. The moon was only a faint sliver, and I had to stick to paths I knew well. Each sound I heard brought with it an image. In the distance, I heard my saddle mare, Prairie Lark, nickering for a friend. For a moment there was no reply, only a whisper of night winds in the bare, creaking branches of the cottonwoods, and the sibilance of icy water over slippery river stones. Then came an answer from Lark's good friend Frosty and soft, muffled hoofbeats as Frosty descended to the river. She stood for a long time as though hoping Lark would cross to her. Then, as Lark nickered again, Frosty answered, and there was the drum of a horse trotting across frozen prairie, and the careful splash of water and tinkle of shore ice as she crossed the Cheyenne River to find her friend.

As she passed me, the wild mare's dappled gray coat took from the faint moonlight the luminescence of a pearl. She shied away as she sensed my presence, then seemed to remember past favors of grain and turned toward me. I touched her forehead briefly and might have scratched her eyelids had not Lark called impatiently. Frosty moved off toward the sound, and soon I heard their soft snuffles of contentment as they wandered off for their night's grazing.

It seemed as though no other wild horses existed on that part of the sanctuary, but suddenly, from a grove of cottonwoods, I heard the squeal of an angry mare and the purrings of a stallion. I was in the wild stallion Painted Desert's territory, and I pictured him there, not a hundred yards off, a sorrel and white, medicine-hat paint, his mane long, flowing almost to his knees.

More horse sounds. My ears were doing double duty, trying to make sense of what my eyes could not see. A dozen mustangs passed me, heading upwards toward bare ridges where the snow had blown into drifts, exposing a rocky slope of frozen grass. There was a sudden snort, as startling in the cold silence as the blast of a buffalo gun, as the lead mare caught my scent and exploded into action. In seconds the whole band was at full gallop, and I heard the snapping of willow branches as they charged through riverine thickets and sought the safety of higher ridges.

It had to be the band of the old buckskin mare I call Ghost Dancer. In her seventeen years here at the sanctuary she has never come to accept me. She bears a rifle bullet in her hip from her early life in the Nevada desert, and that has taught her that humans are never to be trusted. More sounds from her band: a call from an old mare to a friend separated in the charge up the hillside, a cough from the ancient lungs of an elderly animal not used to running.

I sat very still on a rocky ledge and shivered more from excitement than cold. More wild horses came splashing across the river. Much as I wanted to be invisible to the horses and observe their ways, Medicine Hattie found me. I'd saved her life at birth, and she'd imprinted on me. Now she announced my presence with a loud nicker of recognition. She rattled up the hillside and sniffed my pockets for grain, while I cupped my hand over one of her eyes and scratched her lids. More horses joined her, so close I could feel their body heat. Moments later they had edged past me and were gone, and I felt the cold descend from the heights to settle in the valley.

Five minutes stretched to ten. I heard a nervous cry from a colt—more like a scream of distress than a nicker. Stones rattled down the hillside as the young animal followed after Ghost Dancer's herd, looking for its mother. It would have been easy pickings for a cougar. Lonely, it showed me no fear, but sniffed at me curiously until I tried to touch its nose, making it back away and pause just out of reach. I recognized Champagne Lady's colt and remembered his daytime color. He had primitive black bracelets just above his knees, a black stripe down his back from mane to tail set, and his hide bore the smooth, tawny yellow coat of a mountain lion.

There was another rattle of rocks, and the lady herself came back looking for her foal. For one split second as she slid down the hill, I saw the silhouette of her head. Her mouth gaped open and her ears were laid back in anger. I shoved the colt toward her.

The mare must have known my scent for she stopped, sniffed her baby, and moved up a step so the colt could nurse. The little colt squealed in apparent delight and lost no time suckling in the darkness.

I could hear the herd near me. A trim hoof striking rock sounds a blunt bell. Far down the hill, a lonely mare nickers for a friend separated somehow during the night's grass-to-grass wanderings, and the black shape nearest me answers back. From the crest of a hill, a mustang coughs the night dust from clotted lungs, and there are snufflings downslope as animals grow restless with a sense of the coming change from obscurity of vision to full sight. The horses are black shapes in the dark, invisible yet surrounded by a field of warmth and energy that keeps me from colliding with them, like a soft wall warning that I am too close.

How marvelous to watch another dawn come up over the wild-horse herd! The moment comes suddenly when the white horses take first shape—scattered blobs of remnant moonlight, luminescent pearls on the hillside that vanish intermittently as dark forms drift between them and me. Palominos appear; then light buckskins, sorrels, and roans; then bays and blacks. The herd takes form in a pinkish dawn. I can almost read the horses' thoughts as grazing buddies come together at the edge of the herd and drift away together like couples leaving a bar at midnight, hoping the rest of the herd won't notice and follow. I hear the soft sounds of a foal nursing its mother and slip down toward the river so as not to disturb its breakfast. It is almost daylight, but the light of a lantern still glows faintly from a window of the old prairie house I call home.

THE TOUGHNESS OF THE MUSTANGS
HELPS THEM SURVIVE THROUGH HARSH WINTERS.

THICK WINTER COATS PROVIDE ESSENTIAL PROTECTION
FROM WIND, SNOW, AND COLD.

WHEN WATER FREEZES,
A WILD HORSE
WILL BREAK THE ICE
WITH A HOOF SO HE
CAN DRINK.

ICY WINTER WINDS
CAN LOWER THE
TEMPERATURE TO
BELOW ZERO
FOR WEEKS AT A TIME.

LAYERS OF LONG HAIR ON THIS YEARLING
PROTECT HIM FROM THE COLD.

FOOD CHOICES CHANGE WITH THE SEASONS,
AND WILD HORSES ADAPT TO DIFFERENT DIETS.

IN WINTER, HORSES CONSERVE THEIR ENERGY,
RARELY RUNNING FAR.

Above: THICK SNOW MAKES IT HARD FOR MUSTANGS
TO PAW THROUGH FOR GRASS.

Right: WITHOUT MANY PREDATORS, WILD HORSES
OFTEN DIE OF OLD AGE.

SPRING

The wild-horse herds are the first to know when spring has arrived. One day I see them high on the hills overlooking the Cheyenne River, picking around on the small planes of land that are the first to glow in the sun. The wintering grounds where I have fed the horses hay are deserted now, save for a handful of ancient mares that were old when they were shipped to the sanctuary and are nearly twenty years older now.

When winter ends, wild horses go in search of the first new growth of curly buffalo. There is magic to this plant. Each successive dawn finds the horses higher on the hills, seeking the early delicacy. They seem to need its nutritional boost to shed the hairy overcoats of winter and to make the milk flow rich and sweet to their new foals. The winter coats shed quickly. Some of the hair peels off, making carpets around windfalls where the mustangs rub; some hair blows off in the persistent winds and is used as nesting material for birds.

One day the slope that rises above the remains of an ancient Indian village is frozen and austere, the next it is blue with pasque flowers, trembling in the cool wind as though not too sure of their impulse to grow. Chinook winds blow in from the south to send remnant patches of snow cascading into tiny rivers, and I leave my winter jacket hanging in the closet. I see a prairie bumblebee half as big as my thumb working the pasque flowers, carrying a load of yellow pollen from one to another. Then, during the night, the warm winds cease, and the world turns chill again; in the morning, the hills are once again inundated with snow. Unlike buffalo, who hold up their birthing for better weather, the wild mares seem to pick out storms in which to slide their fragile babies, wet and steaming, out into a harsh world. Perhaps it is nature's way of testing the foals, ensuring that only the hardiest will survive this initial test.

Last summer, Painted Desert planted into the mares seeds of color that would grow into this year's foals.

Each spring morning brings new surprises, new foals sliding out of darkness into light. On the morning hillsides, I see mares and foals where there were only mares before. With my binoculars I watch a tiny foal, licked clean as a new shirt, staggering on uncertain legs for balance, seeking out the black, velvety nubs of its mother for the hot, sweet colostrum milk that is filled with magic to fight off infection.

Maybe the mother is Frosty, Prairie Lark, Ghost Dancer, Medicine Hattie, Champagne Lady, or another of those favorites of mine which I have had the impudence to name. They have waited eleven months for their new babies, and each has slipped away from their stallion band to be alone for the event.

There is good reason for their aloneness. Dry mares often try to steal a newborn for themselves, sometimes driving a young, birth-weakened mother away from what is rightfully hers. The poor, confused foal will sometimes follow the dry mare, and each passing hour means that it will have less and less chance of reuniting with its real mother. Without milk, death swiftly follows, and the dry mare often goes off to seek another foal to steal.

In those first hours when a mare is alone with her new foal, bonding comes quickly, and most mares, once they are back on their feet helping the baby to nurse, will fight fiercely against other horses or predators. She stays off alone with her foal until it knows her smell and is safely glued to her side. When mother and offspring eventually rejoin the herd, the other mares go mad with excitement, welcoming the newcomer as though it were the most beautiful foal in the whole world. Let a mare pay too much attention to the newcomer, however, and the mother lays back her ears and charges. Often her hind hooves drum a tattoo on the offender's ribs, and the mother takes her baby out to the edges of the herd and keeps it there until the others show no more interest.

GROUPS MAY INCLUDE SEVERAL GENERATIONS OF MARES WITH THE
HERD STALLION CHANGING EVERY FEW YEARS.

TWO OLD BACHELOR
STALLIONS SPEND ALL
OF THEIR TIME
TOGETHER, RARELY
MORE THAN
A FEW FEET APART.

Once as I was looking for ancient petroglyphs on canyon walls, I came around a rock pillar just as a wild mare was foaling, and the little animal slid wet and steaming into the sunshine, practically at my feet. The mare's head was away from me, and she had evidently had quite a struggle giving birth for she lay quiet and trembling while the baby struggled to free itself from the birth sack. Still immersed in pearly fluid, the baby struck out with tiny yellow hooves as it tried to throw off the sack and get its breath, but to no avail. In a moment it would be too late.

I eased in, removed the sack from its nose, and pumped one front leg to start it breathing. Through the wetness of its rib cage I could see the tiny pulse of a heartbeat. Then it gasped, coughed fluid from its tiny nostrils, and struggled free. The mare lay still, and I stayed too long, not realizing that the little red and white filly was imprinting on me as its mother. Moments later, the mare opened her eyes, looked back, and saw me standing there. Desperately, I tried to slip

away, but the foal struggled to its feet and followed me.

"Go back!" I called—for some strange reason thinking the foal would understand—but on it came, bumping my knees with its rubbery nose to find a place to nurse.

With a squeal of rage the mare leaped from her bed and ran at us, teeth bared. I scrambled out of there with the little foal wobbling along at my side. Just in time I climbed a big rock and sat there out of reach as the mare tried to climb after me, her eyes snapping hatred. She turned to the foal and began sniffing its tail, uncertain at that point whether to love it or hate it. She seemed to forget that I was perched on the rock and began licking her baby, her pink tongue cleaning the remnant fluid from its face and chest. Her udder was distended, and long strands of waxy milk dripped from her dugs, making a white froth on the ground.

The foal knew where I was and kept ignoring the mare, trying to climb the rocks to reach me. I sat perfectly still and watched as the mare attempted to lead the foal away, but finally she gave up and nosed the little animal back along her flanks, where the smell of milk seemed to excite it. For a few moments the foal bumped her rib cage, her brisket, and her front legs with its nose, then finally, as she stepped forward, it found the source and began to nurse.

The little red and white filly was a true medicine hat, with a red cap on its head and a red shield on its chest. Right then and there I named her Medicine Hattie. Having saved her life, I felt a bond with the animal. Medicine-hat horses were sacred to the Indians, who believed that riding such a rare horse into battle made one impervious to arrows or bullets. I saw her frequently as she grew up, and Hattie always seemed to recognize me and was never afraid.

of contentment. But there are realities we must face. We must manage the herd and keep the numbers consistent with vagaries of the weather and the food supply.

Springtime is a time of hard work. There are fences to mend, fallen trees to cut from the roads, and corrals to clean, but it is a joy to work in a light jacket instead of a heavy overcoat. I ride my mustang mare, Prairie Lark, into the backcountry, enjoying each new flower and the emerald green innocence of new grass. The canyons and prairies are filled with birdsong as new arrivals come in from the south. Mountain bluebirds send out scouts to inspect the birdhouses we have placed on fence posts. Killdeer run ahead of us on gravel roads, lark sparrows sing noisily in pursuit of love, and each new foal is a new friend.

Generally, I keep last year's fillies separated from the herd to make sure they get adequate nutrition. In spring I turn them out. They are an independent bunch. A few will seek out their mothers, but most will summer together in the high country, where they will become as skittish as herons, looking for any excuse to spook and run. They find danger in a cougar on a rock or the race of an eagle's shadow as it sails between earth and sun. The flight of raucous pinion jays overhead, the strut of wild turkeys on the morning meadow, and the chatter of a red squirrel in the pine forest all fill the day of yearling wild horses with magic. It will be two years or more before they split up and join older bands. At five they will often have foals of their own, and soon the one horse will become two again.

When I first started the sanctuary, I had only mares and thought that the presence of stallions would only mean management problems. But soon it became apparent that the mares would be happier with a few foals around. Not only do the mares seem possessive about the areas in which their foals were born, but they also seem more satisfied. The foals themselves now have playmates, and the whole atmosphere of the herd is one

HORSES WITH MEDICINE HAT COLORATION WERE SACRED TO NATIVE AMERICANS.

A NEWBORN FOAL
STAYS CLOSE
TO HIS MOTHER,
FREQUENTLY TOUCHING
AND NURSING.

FOALS CAN BE BORN
ANY TIME OF THE
YEAR BUT THOSE BORN
IN LATE SPRING HAVE
A BETTER
CHANCE OF SURVIVAL.

Mares go off by themselves to give birth, then keep
the foal away from the herd for several days to bond with the newborn
and so other mares will not steal her foal.

WITHIN THREE OR FOUR HOURS OF BIRTH, NEWBORNS ARE ABLE
TO FOLLOW THEIR MOTHERS. MOUNTAIN LIONS, AND SOMETIMES COYOTES,
ARE THE ONLY PREDATORS THAT KILL MUSTANG FOALS;
DISEASE AND WINTER STORMS ARE MORE WORRISOME THAN PREDATORS.
THUS, LIFE IS EASY FOR THIS COLT WITH WARM WEATHER, LOTS OF GRASS,
AND PROTECTION BY BEING PART OF A HERD.

MATING IS BRIEF AND USUALLY, BUT NOT ALWAYS,
REQUIRES THE COOPERATION OF THE MARE.

THIS FLEHMEN GRIMACE TELLS A STALLION WHETHER A MARE IS IN ESTRUS.

MUSTANGS KNOW EVERY GULLY AND ESCAPE ROUTE
IN THEIR HOME RANGE SO THE OLDEST MARE CAN LEAD THEM TO SAFETY.

WILD HORSES ARE ALWAYS ALERT
TO SOMETHING NEW OR DIFFERENT AND SOMETIMES CURIOUS
ENOUGH TO COME CLOSER TO INVESTIGATE.

STALLIONS ARE
COSTANTLY PROVING
THEIR STRENGTH TO
EACH OTHER.
THEY COMMUNICATE
BY SNIFFING, PUSHING,
SHOVING, AND
BRUSHING AGAINST
EACH OTHER.

STALLIONS WITHOUT MARES FORM A HIERARCHY
WITHOUT SERIOUS FIGHTING.

In serious fights between herd stallions, they sometimes back up to each other and kick with hind legs. As one horse's legs hit the ground, the other horse's hooves fly.

REAL BATTLES BETWEEN HERD STALLIONS ARE BRIEF AND SAVAGE
AND LEAVE SCARS, AS SEEN ON THE SIDE OF THIS HORSE.

SUMMER

All spring, mysterious forces make the mustangs of the Black Hills Wild Horse Sanctuary look longingly west toward Oregon, Nevada, and Wyoming where they were born and ran free until captured by agents of the government. Years of living in peace on the sanctuary have not quelled their instinct to return to the home range where they were born. As the season changes to summer, the horses face another reality: insects.

A succession of fly species changes the mustang's behavior in the summertime. It is the nature of a wild horse to try to outrun the threat of danger. Manes and tails streaming in the wind, they dash across the grasslands, foals glued to their sides, trying to leave the torment behind.

Trailing in pursuit come face flies, deerflies, stable flies, nose flies, botflies, and green-and-white-headed horseflies, to name a few. Each fly species has a different strategy and elicits a different defense mechanism in a herd of wild horses.

The mustangs seek the high places, where a friendly wind keeps the flies hidden in the grass. They pair up nose to tail, each using its tail to knock the flies off the other. I know when nose flies are about because horses trot and even lope with noses close to the grass to brush off flies and prevent them from laying eggs in their nostrils. Nose flies operate close to the ground, so one horse will drape its head over another's neck or back, keeping it above the level of a nose fly's territory. Heel flies set up stations and wait for an unsuspecting critter to pass, choosing the horse's heels as the spot to lay their eggs, which will enter the body and end up as grubs or warbles on the animal's back. Slow, bumbling botflies glue their yellow eggs to a horse's coat, and they end up invading the digestive system when the horse grooms itself with its teeth.

To escape the insects, wild horses wallow in the mud of a water hole and retreat, their sides shining with a protective coat of mud. Carrying the mud to the top of a distant knoll, they shake off the coating in a cloud of dust, unaware that they have made the wallow imperceptibly deeper and able to hold more water.

The water hole is important to herds all year long, but especially so in the summer. Lead mares determine where and when the band will go to drink or graze, while the stallion usually trails behind to guard from incursions by rival stallions. Often he will keep his thirsty mares waiting atop a knoll until rival bands have drunk their fill and the coast is clear. The lead mare descends to water first, leading the other mares, while the stallion follows, sniffing at the manure piles left by others. He stands astride the piles and urinates and defecates on them, trying to mask the scent and mark the water hole as his very own.

Once the lead mare decides it is safe to drink, she wades in, nose thrust forward, followed by the others. They drink deeply then head for shallower water where they paw the water with one front hoof, sending up big gouts of muddy water. Some roll in the shallows and laze about until the lead mare decides their time is up. Off they go, often at a gallop, until they have attained a comfort zone where clouds sweep their backs and they feel safe once more.

Sometimes in the summertime I move the animals from areas where the grass is becoming short, so they can better feed. The horses know me well. They allow me to bump along behind them in my battered old pickup truck. The mares with new foals have minds of their own and are apt to quit the herd, taking off like a strand of a woman's hair in the wind. I try to anticipate their moves and head them off, tucking them back into the herd. Time and again they try me, until the herd begins to shape up and move as though of a single mind.

I'm wise to their ways. When they come to a hill, they will invariably circle the hill on me and try to escape. I cut across and am there in front of them. Resignedly they turn back and seem a little embarrassed that I have figured out their ploy.

Horses drive best uphill, and suddenly they are traveling fast, heading for the higher country where I wanted them to go. Bays, sorrels, blacks, grays, paints, roans—all in a churn of color. There is a heady smell of crushed sage, the rumble of hooves as the ground trembles beneath them, the nickering of one friend to another and of a foal for its mother.

I have named many of these animals, for they are like family to me. The lead mare in this group is Yuskeya, which means *freedom* in the Sioux language. A big dappled gray, whose hairy fetlocks show her draft-horse ancestry, she has never accepted my friendship. Now she pauses atop a headland and turns to look back, like a general surveying a battle. Her troops sweep on beneath her. Frosty dashes by, crop-eared from a Nevada winter long ago, dapples fading to solid iron gray. Supermare's white stockings flash as she runs. Magnificent Mary, huge headed and angular, makes little test excursions of her own as she tries to get others to follow. I see Cirrus, feet hardly touching the ground, sprinting ahead of the others in pure joy; Painted Lady, colored red and white like no other; Lark, with her new jet-black foal; Funny Face, her coat gleaming like burnished ebony. Again and again I count the marker horses, making sure that none have split from the herd and that I have them all.

As I drive through the pine forest, I lose sight of the horses but know that they will carry to the open plains ahead. Just as I skirt the last fallen tree with my truck, I see them scattered on the vast plain. Heads down, they are grazing. Only Yuskeya is standing with her head up, watching me from afar, assessing the danger.

Gray clouds in the distance drop a skein of summer rain. I drive back through a range empty and lonely without horses. They will return in good season when the grass has grown up again and gone to seed.

WHEN A HERD INCLUDES STALLIONS OF UNUSUAL COLORATION,
THE WHOLE HERD BECOMES MORE COLORFUL WITHIN JUST A FEW YEARS.

THIS COLORFUL RUNNING HERD IS MOSTLY MADE UP OF PINTOS.

AT FIRST, A FOAL'S
ONLY CONSTANT
COMPANION IS HIS
MOTHER, BUT AS DAYS
GO BY, THE FOAL WILL
EXPLORE HIS NEW
ENVIRONMENT.
AS FOALS FROLIC, THEY
DEVELOP STRENGTH
AND AGILITY—OFTEN
BY PLAYING
WITH EACH OTHER.

ALL THE DAYS OF PLAY PAY OFF WHEN A WILD HORSE
NEEDS TO RUN TO ESCAPE DANGER.

IF THE WATER SOURCE
IS LARGE ENOUGH,
WILD HORSES
PREFER TO WALK INTO
THE WATER
BEFORE DRINKING.

A STALLION KICKS UP
THE WATER BEFORE
DRINKING, PERHAPS TO
GET RID OF INSECTS.

GESTATION LASTS ELEVEN MONTHS AND MARES HAVE FOALS EVERY YEAR; THEIR NORMAL STATE IS PREGNANCY.

AUTUMN

Suddenly, one night after the heat of August, the coolness comes. The wild horses range farther, investigating rocky steeps of ungrazed grasses, feeding for longer hours, and laying on fat for winter. The foals venture away from their mothers, seeking companionship with others their age.

There is not much play in a mother mare. During the summer she gave all her energy to a demanding foal that clung to her side like a shadow on a sunny day. In vain the foals tried to tease their mothers into playing games. Now the foals race across the prairie, the rocky ground beating hardness into their tiny hooves. They are leaping gullies, prancing, dancing, acting silly, and staging mock battles—tails high, bursting with energy. Sporting, they chew on each other's manes or rise together on hind legs like fighting stallions.

The first frosts turn the cottonwood trees along the Cheyenne River to golden, and, as transpiration ceases along miles of river in South Dakota and Wyoming, the river rises to three times its summer volume. The wild horses invade the willow thickets, sampling golden leaves and splashing in the shallows along the river. Gone from their coats is the sheen of summer as they put on the thick, heavy-haired trappings of winter. Like humans wearing bulky sweaters, they look larger than they really are.

With autumn's approach, it is time to relieve the mares of the heavy demands their foals make upon them and give these mothers time to put on condition before winter. One of the fields along the Cheyenne is a natural gathering place for the horses. Here I have built drift fences so I can ease the wild horses into a lane that leads off the mountain, down across the headquarters flats, and into our wild-horse corrals. There is no need for helicopters or cowboys on horseback to chase the animals, no need to frighten them. I wait until there are no people around, then drift them off the hill and into the corrals, where we have set out rewards of sweet feed.

Separating the foals from their mothers can be dangerous, and as I walk into a narrow lane filled with nervous mares and their inexperienced offspring, I rely on good help to run the gates behind me. Basically, I let the mares slip past me and hold the foals. The mares have gone through the operation before and are quick to take their freedom and dash past. Once a few mares have passed me down the lane, a helper opens a gate and lets them into a larger corral. If a colt runs by me by mistake, it is shunted into a holding corral along the lane. The colts are nervous without their mothers, but soon find their pals of summer in the holding pen and settle down. Wild horses that share dramatic experiences such as being captured or hauled in a trailer together often form bonds that last for the rest of their lives. The foals that are thrown together at weaning time are sometimes difficult to separate.

Timing of the weaning is important. If we wean too early in the fall, there is still a strong bond between the foal and its mother. When the time is right, there is independence about the relationship, and the mothers seem relieved to be separated from the weanlings, who are perhaps six months old. When all the mares are pared from the herd of foals, we turn the mares out of the corral. They thunder down the lane to freedom and are soon in the backcountry, with nary a good-bye nicker to the foals who, by now, are playing quite happily with their pals.

While I have felt that older wild horses never become completely happy in captivity, no matter how well they are treated, the weanlings quickly adjust and readily make friends with the humans in their lives. A professional is able to train even a fifteen-year-old mustang to ride, but the average person who adopts a wild horse from the Bureau of Land Management would do better acquiring a foal.

Modern training methods, such as those taught by Pat Parelli and several others, are a vast improvement

INSECTS PLAGUE MUSTANGS
DURING THE HEAT OF SUMMER.

over the ways of my youth, which roughly consisted of taking advantage of a horse, sacking him out a few times, slapping a saddle on his back, and hanging tough in the saddle until the animal quit bucking. The new methods are wonderfully gentle and much easier, not only on the colt but also on the trainer. The end result is an animal who is safe and obedient, yet a good friend.

While there are many wild-horse adoption success stories, where the horses become wonderful companion and riding horses, I am sobered by the fact that last year alone we took in over fifty horses that were adopted from the Bureau of Land Management only to be returned by folks who cared for them but lacked the knowledge to handle them. They loved those horses enough to pay transportation costs from Oregon, California, and even Florida, but breathed a sigh of relief when they watched the horses thunder through our gate to freedom.

In captivity, those wild horses had hoodwinked the owners and developed bad attitudes. Some of them were even dangerously pushy. We turned them loose into the wild herds, where they generally had a hard time adjusting to the other horses and tried to dominate.

The wild, free life shapes a horse in ways we do not yet understand. However well trained a wild horse becomes; no matter how skilled he is in dressage, jumping, cutting, reining, roping, team penning, or trail riding; no matter how many silver cups and ribbons he wins; if he has spent a certain amount of time in freedom, he will always remember, and a certain sadness will be evident when one looks into his eyes.

The foals in the corrals, so recently weaned, are quick to adjust. Much of their fright has been learned by watching how their mothers react to outside influences. We place a gentle mare with them, and the babies soon notice that this surrogate mother shows no fear of humans. I consider my hours standing among them, walking away from them when they show interest or feigning disinterest in them completely, well spent. Soon I can touch them and do all the grooming techniques horses do to themselves—rubbing their sweet spots, kneading their manes, and scratching their cheeks, tail sets, and itchy chests.

Like human children, wild foals play games. Their favorite is king of the mountain, where one foal climbs to a vantage point in the corral and shoulders everyone else off. They race each other to the end of the corral and back, or dash off trying to get the others to follow.

The fillies will be turned back into the herd to replace the old animals, which are now part of the coyotes and eagles that patrol the land. The colts will be sold to new homes, since the sanctuary is a charity that must find every means for support. I watch the trailers drive up the road to civilization with heavy heart. But every colt that leaves here is helping the remaining horses run free.

AT ONE TIME, ALL THE MUSTANGS WERE FROM SPANISH HORSES
BUT BLOODLINES HAVE BEEN DILUTED IN MOST PLACES
SINCE NORTHERN EUROPEAN HORSES HAVE JOINED THE HERDS.

Two to five million mustangs
roamed the American West in the 1800s.

THIS MUSTANG BEARS SORRAIA COLORATION
WITH A BI-COLORED MANE AND TAIL.

BACHELOR BUDDIES STAY TOGETHER OR MOVE
FROM GROUP TO GROUP OF BACHELOR STALLIONS.

IN A HARSH
ENVIRONMENT, NATURE
WEEDS OUT THE
WEAKER HORSES SO
ONLY THE
STRONG, AGILE, AND
WARY SURVIVE.

THE BEAUTY OF THE PRAIRIE IS ONLY MADE BETTER
WHEN THERE ARE MUSTANGS IN IT.

A WILD STALLION WILL BREAK DOWN FENCES TO STEAL
DOMESTIC MARES FOR HIS HAREM.

THROUGH THE GENERATIONS, MUSTANGS HAVE BECOME SMALLER IN HARSH HABITATS
BECAUSE SMALL HORSES REQUIRE LESS FOOD.

NATURAL SELECTION HAS MADE WILD HORSE HOOVES HARD;
A LAME HORSE CANNOT SURVIVE RUNNING ON ROCKS AND HARD GROUND.

STALLIONS WILL DRIVE THEIR OFFSPRING OUT
OF THE HERD BY AGE TWO OR THREE.

By dividing into harems and having a home range, wild horses
are less likely to overgraze the land.

SURVIVAL INSTINCT
SENDS THIS HERD
FLYING THROUGH
SAGEBRUSH-COVERED
HILLS.

DAYS OF WONDER

One winter night, when temperatures held at twenty below zero, I was driving back from the town of Hot Springs when my pickup truck failed me some six miles from the sanctuary. There was no traffic on that lonely road, and I left the truck to walk home.

There was no moonlight, and I had to guess where the edges of the highway gave way to the slopes of the borrow pit. Despite the wind, which seemed to sap every bit of warmth from my body, I pushed forward and managed to turn off the main road onto the sanctuary. Nearing exhaustion, all I could think about was sitting down in the snow to rest.

Just as I came close to giving up, I heard muffled hoofbeats in the snow. I strained to see in the darkness, but the world was as black as the inside of a cow. Suddenly, a band of perhaps thirty wild horses surrounded me, their bodies shielding me from the wind. I heard the crisp rasping of their hooves on frozen snow and sensed that I was probably in a good position to get kicked or stepped on, but there was little I could do but push on down the road.

I kept bumping up against a mustang on my left, yet the animal did nothing to move away. Risking everything I put one hand up under its mane and warmed it, then the other. Another horse crowded me from the right and I walked forward like a blind man between two friends. I sensed that I was in the middle of the herd, and all the wild horses were protecting me as though I were a foal.

The road soon turned sharply to the left, and the animals turned with it. For a moment at the next bend the group thinned and the icy winds tore at me, but then the animals moved closer as though to shield me. We went for another half mile until we came to a cattle guard in the middle of the road over which they could not pass. As suddenly as they had appeared, they were gone again in the night.

I have never been able to explain what happened that night. Horses do have a tendency to join traveling animals, whether deer or other horses. Perhaps they were merely joining me for a hike. Maybe they were protecting me by keeping me in the center of the herd. Whatever the reason, they most likely saved my life.

Not long after that bewildering experience, I was tending to some foals in the corrals when I heard horses running. The sanctuary manager and I climbed a fence, looked off across the fields, and saw what we thought was a pack of dogs harassing a herd of wild horses. Running as fast as we could, we gained the pasture only to find that the dogs were actually coyotes. The animals were trying to kill a yearling mule deer, and the horses were trying to run the coyotes away. As we approached, the band of mares made a tight circle around the deer and kept the coyotes at bay.

I attempted to move the deer into the adjoining fence corner where I could examine its wounds, but the mares threatened me, lowering their heads and weaving toward me like herding stallions as I approached. They laid back their ears in anger, and I moved away. When I next looked back, the deer had headed down the slope to the river, and the mares were already headed back up to the hills to graze.

When the wild horses protected me that cold, windy night, they were perhaps exhibiting the same behavior patterns they showed in protecting the deer against coyotes. This behavior is present in other animals including the musk ox. Long ago I penned the lines:

> The musk ox knows what snow and ice is,
> Shows this behavior in crises.
> When wolves come hunting them for dinner
> They form a circle, babies inner.

Other happenings on the sanctuary, however, cannot be explained. A few years ago, one of my marker horses, a beautiful black and white animal we named

THIS DAPPLE GRAY STALLION STRUTS WITH TAIL RAISED, ENJOYING HIS FREEDOM.

Mrs. B, disappeared from the group in which she normally ran. The back part of the sanctuary is essentially roadless, and it was there that I looked for Mrs. B but to no avail. Three years passed, but there was still no sign of the animal.

One day, as I was relaxing in front of our tourist center, I saw movement at the mouth of Hell Canyon, just across from where I sat. I stood up for a better look, but there was nothing. That night a group of horses came in to the stack yards to feed on our winter hay supply, but they were gone by morning.

The next day I looked up from my work to see a black horse watching me carefully from the mouth of the canyon. The animal had a white blaze and looked suspiciously like Mrs. B.

There was a full moon that night, and I sat in my truck watching the stacks of hay to see which horses were stealing in to feed. It was nearly midnight when I saw movement, and out of the shadows stepped Mrs. B, followed by her two-year-old filly and a yearling.

For two weeks, Mrs. B hid out in the mouth of the canyon and watched my activities. And then, one morning, I checked the stack yard and found it undisturbed. But there were tracks and wet spots along the riverbank where a group of horses had crossed from the far side, and tracks in the sand where three horses had traveled up the road. The tracks led past the stack yard without stopping, then turned down the lane leading to the corrals. I followed along slowly, careful not to frighten my quarry.

There standing quietly in the center of the corral were Mrs. B's two foals, while beside them on the ground lay Mrs. B. She had come home to die and brought her babies with her. 🐎

STALLIONS POSTURE AND SNORT,
SIZING UP THE OPPONENT.

STILL WET FROM ROLLING IN A WATERHOLE,
TWO STALLIONS REAR IN BATTLE.

HORSES SNORT TO CLEAR THEIR NOSTRILS,
IMPROVING THEIR ABILITY TO SMELL.

THIS PAINT STALLION IS OF OVARO
COLORATION—A SOLID COAT WITH WHITE SPLASHES.

SILHOUETTES OF HORSES STAND ATOP A HILL
AT THE BLACK HILLS WILD HORSE SANCTUARY.

WHEN IT RAINS, MUSTANGS USUALLY STOP THEIR GRAZING
AND JUST STAND STILL, LOOKING MISERABLE.

Chapter 6

THE TRUE WORTH OF WILD HORSES

ASK A HUNDRED PEOPLE whether or not wild horses are important to America, and you will get a hundred different answers. Those who have an investment in the grasslands of the West or raise registered horses might regale you with horror stories about how wild horses trample winter wheat, muddy up water holes, turn grasslands into deserts, breed like prairie dogs, and have deteriorated in quality to the point where they are a discredit to the horse's name and do little more than cost the taxpayers of this great land a lot of money that could be better spent taking care of human poor.

Talk to someone who has had the good fortune to ride a fine mustang and the answer, of course, will be far different.

During the 1800s, there were perhaps two million mustangs running wild and free across North America's western plains. Western settlement and barbed-wire fences around productive land and water sources put an end to huge herds. Many captured wild horses died in battle during the two World Wars; others were killed for human consumption or went to feed pets or poultry. Development projects such as those around Reno,

Nevada, stole acre after acre of wild-horse range. Naturally occurring droughts dried up some of the few remaining water holes left to horses and put them in direct competition with cattle and sheep for water and grass.

Had it not been for cattlemen and Indians, the remaining horse herds might have dwindled to almost nothing. Both groups had a stake in the wild herds as a source of riding animals. In tough winters, many a rancher—Indian and white—opened their gates to wild herds and fed them hay, ensuring their survival. Wild-horse runners kept the bands moving to fresh feed and water, mixed the bands so that inbreeding was not a factor, and prevented inferior animals from breeding mares. When herd numbers began to grow, however, so did the pressures for their capture.

Critics of the wild horse make much of the fact that there have been vast infusions of domestic blood into the horse herds. The government released remount stallions into wild herds to create better horses for the cavalry. When ranchers opted for tractors instead of teams of draft horses, it was common practice to turn their surplus animals out on the ranges, where they were soon absorbed into wild herds. Most wild herds today do indeed show traces of domestic stock, but such introductions have only a short-term effect on wild herds, as it is the short-bodied, tough, mustang types that survive and live on to reproduce, while other influences fade. There are individuals in any herd that resemble the horses brought to the Americas by Portuguese and Spanish explorers.

Opponents of the wild horse are also critical because the horse is an introduced species from domesticated stock. The fact is, horses originated in the Americas and were here long before the first hominids arrived. Domestication has not altered the spirit and personality of the horse, although it has deprived them of their uniformity. Before one derides the wild horse and its importance to our history, one must consider just how humans would have survived in North America without the horse—first as a source of food, then as much more.

For America's native population, nothing was more important to their well-being than horses and bison. Had the whites not made a major campaign to kill off Indian horses, some tribes might have fought the encroachment of settlers for another fifty years.

Certainly, no animal was as important as the horse for the settling of North America, and wild-horse herds provided a major source of animals for riding and drayage. If the mustangs themselves were too small for heavier work, they crossed readily with larger horses, producing animals with great stamina, good feet, good minds, and an ability to maintain body condition on minimum forage.

It was the horse that made a heroic figure of the American cowboy and made possible the development of a great beef industry. Picture a cowboy roping a wild steer without a horse, or men afoot driving great trail herds across the West to market. Often horses were the only practical means of transportation for individuals and armies. They deserve respect and protection for their great contribution to our history.

Raising horses is still a major American industry, but horses have become specialized, as breeds for specific uses, such as jumping, trail and endurance riding, dressage, racing, polo, cutting, barrel racing, and other rodeo events, were developed. The American quarter horse was developed for quarter-mile racing, but its muscular build and varied abilities made it a natural for many other uses. It has become America's all-around horse. But most quarter horses go back to a handful of early stallions and suffer from close breeding. Already some lines of quarter horses are victims of skeletal breakdowns and skin disorders, and ailments of the nervous system may follow.

Where will the quarter-horse industry turn for new blood? Our wild-horse herds are a great genetic resource just waiting to be tapped. Proper selection from the vast gene pools available can bring the quarter-horse industry hybrid vigor, stamina, good health, good feet, and good bones. It can also bring back something lost to horses through intensive breeding: smarts.

The time is coming when the pressure on western ranges will become more and more intense, as human populations grow and true wilderness becomes harder to find. Wild horses will need some form of human management, such as sanctuaries, to survive.

Drawing on my years of experience with wild horses and the Black Hills sanctuary, I have a new concept that might help wild horses everywhere. It would require large areas set aside specifically for wild horses and fenced with a system of drift fences, so the wild-horse herds could be gathered quietly without being chased by helicopters. The foals would be removed at weaning time, and replacement fillies added as needed to maintain both quality and numbers in the herd. Stallions would be removed during non-breeding months and run separately on their own section of the range. They would be supplied to the mares in the spring as needed to maintain a controlled production, but no more foals would be produced than adoption demands could handle. Herd numbers would be determined by very conservative estimates of range conditions and forage

MUSTANGS RUN
THROUGH THE
BARRENS OF ADOBE
TOWN, WYOMING.

supply, while the utmost care would be given to prevent inbreeding.

Granted, I would like to see a return to the conditions of my youth a half century ago, when wild horses were truly free, when nature selected what would survive and what would perish, when mares had a surplus of stallions from which to chose their mates, when predators kept the herds from destroying their range, and when wild horses were quality animals prized by ranchers and other horsemen concerned with their welfare. But times have changed dramatically in the West. Development is widespread, and once-lonely vistas are now paved over with yard-to-yard housing and shopping malls that will never grow an orange or an ear of corn. We will have to learn to accept only a part of what life once was, but we must never forget the beauty and importance of our wild horses and their right to run wild and free.

I can sense this freedom when I watch bands of mustangs thundering across this prairie haven for no other reason than the pure joy coursing through their veins. There are no sad-eyed horses here. The music of drumming hooves echoes from ancient rimrocks, then dies with the distance. I whisper to myself a long-remembered line from John Keats's "Ode to a Nightingale": "Fled is that music—do I wake or sleep?" 🐎

A WILD HORSE RUNNING WITH MANE AND TAIL FLYING
IS POETRY IN MOTION. BEAVER RIM, WYOMING.

"A HORSE IS WORTH MORE THAN RICHES." —*Spanish proverb*

"THE WIND
OF HEAVEN IS THAT
WHICH BLOWS
BETWEEN A
HORSE'S EARS."
—*Arabian proverb*

THE END OF THE RAINBOW IS IN COUNTRY WHERE WILD HORSES LIVE.
LANDER WILD HORSE MANAGEMENT AREA, WYOMING.

WITHIN A GROUP OF
HORSES, CLOSENESS,
TOUCHING, AND SIGNS
OF AFFECTION ARE
COMMON. ARROWHEAD
MOUNTAIN, MONTANA.

"I THINK THAT WILD
HORSES HAVE MORE
SECRETS THAN GENTLE
ONES." —J. Frank
Dobie, *The Mustangs*

AS HUMAN POPULATIONS GROW,
WILD HORSES NEED FURTHER CARE AND MANAGEMENT,
INCLUDING SANCTUARIES.

"THE HORSE IS GOD'S GIFT TO MAN." —*Arabian proverb*

INDEX

A

Adobe Town, Wyoming, 197
Andalusians, 94
Andoni Plain, Namibia, 48, 50
Arrowhead Mountain, Montana,
    24, 30, 203
Assateague Island, 100–114
Aus, Namibia, 62, 64, 65, 67–69

B

Beaver Rim, Wyoming, 129, 198
Biddle, Margaret, 22
Bitter Creek, Wyoming, 120
Black Hills, 119
Black Hills wild Horse Sanctuary,
    South Dakota, 94, 120, 121
Bloomsfield, Nebraska, 120
Bonaparte, Napoleon, 83
Brislawn, Robert, 94
Buffalo Creek, Wyoming, 125
Bureau of Land Management
    wild-horse area, 95
Burns Amendment, 121

C

Camargue Horse, 78–93
Carmody Lake, Wyoming, 21, 32,
    33, 130
Cheyenne River, 119, 133, 135, 144,
    170
Chiloquin, Oregon, 118
Chincoteague Island, 100–114
Chobe Park, Botswana, 53
Columbus, Christopher, 36
Conant Creek, Wyoming, 124, 128
Corolla Island,
    North Carolina, 112
Crooks Mountain, Wyoming, 26
Custer National Forest,
    Montana, 23, 40
Cyclone Rim, Wyoming, 131

D

Dartmoor Pony, 77
Deep Creek, 22, 23
Divide Basin, Wyoming, 30
Dobie, J. Frank, 203

E

Eohippus, 35
Estes, Richard Despard, 44
Etosha National Park, Namibia,
    45, 46, 48, 50, 52, 54, 56
Exmoor Pony, 74

F

Farnsworth, Mamie, 22, 23
Fields, Slim, 23
Flint Hills, Oklahoma, 119
Ford Motor Company, 121
Fuego Mountain, 22

G

Garub, Namibia, 62, 66
Godebski, 78

H

Hell Canyon, 187
Henry, Marguerite, 100, 101
Hot Springs, 186

I

Icelandic Pony, 92, 93

J

Johnston, Velma,
    "Wild Horse Annie", 117

K

Keats, John, 197
Kiger Mustangs, 95, 98
Klamath Indian Reservation, 19
Kuntz, Frank and Leo, 95

L

Lander Wild Horse Management
    Area, Wyoming, 122, 123, 202
Lander, Wyoming, 127
Lewa Down, Kenya, 58
Lusitanos, 94

M

Michelson, George, 119
Mistral, Frederic, 84
Misty of Chincoteague, 100, 101
Mount Rushmore, 119
Mounta Mazama, 36

N

Namib Desert, 57, 62–77
New Forest Pony, 75
Nokota Mustangs, 95

P

Parelli, Pat, 170
Percheron, 95
Pinto, 163
Powers, Stephanie, 121
Pryor Mountain Mustangs, 94, 95
Pryor Mountains, Montana, 25, 40,
    94, 96, 97
Przewalski Horse, 70, 71
Puget, Denise, 78

R

Red Desert, Wyoming, 28, 29
Remington, Frederic, 95
Rhone Delta, 78
Rosebud Indian Reservation,
    South Dakota, 121

S

Salt Wells Creek, Wyoming,
    119, 127
Samburu National Reserve,
    Kenya, 45, 46
Sandwash Basin, Colorado, 27
Somali Wild Ass, 60
Sorraia Wild Horse, 72, 73, 94,
    95, 174
South Dakota Community
    Foundation, 119
Spanish Mustang Registry, 94
Sycan River, 21

T

The Mustangs, 203
Theodore Roosevelt National
    Park, 95
Thoroughbred, 62, 68, 95

W

Watt, Susan, 120
Wild Horse and Burro Protection
    Act of 1971, 117, 118, 121, 129
Wildhorse Meadow, 22
Wildhorse Springs, 22
Williamson River, 19, 23, 121

Y

Yamsay Mountain, 23

Z

Zebras, 43–61
    Grevy, 43, 45, 46, 58
    Hartmann's Mountain, 43, 54,
      56, 57
    Plains, 43, 46, 53

ABOUT THE AUTHORS

AUTHOR Dayton O. Hyde is an old-time cowboy as well as a former rodeo rider and rodeo clown. In the 1980s, he witnessed some of America's surviving wild mustangs being rounded up and sent to slaughter; it pulled at his heart strings, and he vowed to do something about it. In 1988, he established The Black Hills Wild Horse Sanctuary near Hot Springs, South Dakota, an 11,000-acre ranch to protect wild horses. Long held sacred by the Cheyenne, Lakota, and other Native American tribes, the area is a place where visitors can view the Wild West as it was. Dayton is also the photographer and author of fifteen other books on cowboying, fishing, and natural history; his most recent is the critically acclaimed memoir, *The Pastures of Beyond.*

PHOTOGRAPHERS Rita and Charles Summers have traveled the globe photographing wild horses. Their work has been published in numerous books and magazines, including *National Geographic*, *Audubon*, *Sierra*, *BBC Wildlife*, *Natural History*, *Nature Conservancy*, *Orion*, *Outdoor Photographer*, *People*, and *Ranger Rick.* They live in Parker, Colorado.

CENTRAL ARKANSAS LIBRARY SYSTEM
SIDNEY S. McMATH BRANCH LIBRARY
LITTLE ROCK, ARKANSAS